ARTIE SHAW

Also available from Continuum:

ARTIE SHAW

His Life and Music

JOHN WHITE

continuum
NEW YORK • LONDON

2004

The Continuum International Publishing Group Inc
15 East 26 Street, New York, NY 10010

The Continuum International Publishing Group Ltd
The Tower Building, 11 York Road, London SE1 7NX

www.continuumbooks.com

Copyright © 1998, 2004 by John White

Originally published in Great Britain in 1998 by The University of Hull Press.
Revised edition published in 2004 by Continuum, by arrangement with Bayou
Press Ltd.

Printed in the United States of America

Library of Congress Cataloging-in-Publication Data

White, John, 1939 Feb. 5–
    Artie Shaw : his life and Music / John White.— rev. ed.
        p.   cm.
    Includes bibliographical references and index.
    ISBN 0-8264-6915-9 (pbk. : alk. paper)
    1. Shaw, Artie, 1910–   2. Jazz musicians—United States—Biography.
I. Title.
ML419.S52W45   2004
788.6′2165′092—dc22   2004000473

CONTENTS

She knows exactly how many times everybody's been divorced and why, and how many Warner brothers there are. She even knows how many times Artie Shaw's been married, which I bet he couldn't tell you himself. She asked me if I had ever married Artie Shaw, and when I said No, seemed to think I was pulling her leg or must have done it without noticing. I tried to explain that when a girl goes to Hollywood, she doesn't have to marry Artie Shaw, it's optional, but I don't think I convinced her.

P. G. Wodehouse, *The Mating Season* (1949)

I suppose Artie was the first intelligent, intellectual man I'd ever met, and he bowled me over. I remember that the first time he took me to a little Italian restaurant across from RKO studios. Artie looked across at me and said, "Ava, I think that physically, emotionally, and mentally you are the most perfect woman I've ever met." His eyes never moved from mine, and he went on, "And what's more, I'd marry you tonight, except for the fact that I've married too many wives already." Artie took it for granted that everyone was panting to marry Artie Shaw.

Ava Gardner, *Ava: My Story* (1990)

Artie Shaw was a great clarinet player, but I never felt he generated the intensive drive that Benny Goodman did. At first, his band was a spin-off from the Goodman approach, but some of the things he did with strings were very rewarding. Artie had no sense of humor, in my opinion, and always took himself too seriously to suit me.

Charlie Barnet, *Those Swinging Years* (1984)

For Teresa

THE ARTIE SHAW STORY

BEGIN THE BEGUINE
STAR DUST
DANCING IN THE DARK
OH, LADY BE GOOD
CONCERTO FOR CLARINET
NIGHTMARE
SMOKE GETS IN YOUR EYES
MY BLUE HEAVEN
ALL THE THINGS YOU ARE
SUMMERTIME
ST. JAMES INFIRMARY
FRENESI

PREFACE TO
SECOND EDITION

As the dashing and handsome leader of one of America's most accomplished big bands in the 1930s and 1940s, Artie Shaw achieved measures of fame and fortune which for a time eclipsed even those of his great rival, Benny Goodman. According to one estimate, Shaw's five top single recordings had sold over 65 million copies by 1965, and he has calculated that by 1990, his total sales topped 100 million records. In 1962 at a special ceremony in New York, Shaw received Golden Disc awards for his million-seller records: *Begin the Beguine, Nightmare, Traffic Jam, Dancing in the Dark, Stardust, Summit Ridge Drive,* and *Back Bay Shuffle.* All of them feature Shaw's superlative clarinet playing, remarkable for its plangent tone and astonishing technical facility. Unlike Goodman, who has been the subject of two recent and well-researched biographies—James Lincoln Collier's *Benny Goodman and the Swing Era* (1990), and Ross Firestone's *Swing, Swing, Swing: The Life & Times of Benny Goodman* (1993)—Shaw has not received comparable treatment by any jazz historian. This book is intended to remedy that omission.

Born in 1910, Shaw became—and remains—a controversial, contradictory, and enigmatic figure. Between 1936 and 1955 he organized and led at least eight different bands and small groups, some of which were dissolved in acrimonious circumstances. An early and avid seeker of material success, Shaw on three notable occasions declared that he was temperamentally unsuited to the role of public celebrity, and abandoned his career as a professional musician to follow a variety of pursuits: writer, farmer, fisherman, marksman, film distributor, broadcaster, lecturer, architect, and student of the classical guitar. For five years he lived in self-imposed exile in Spain. Married eight times, his wives included film stars Lana Turner and Ava Gardner, Elizabeth Kern (daughter of songwriter Jerome Kern), Doris Dowling, Kathleen Winsor (author of the salacious novel *Forever Amber*), and actress Evelyn Keyes. (When asked why he married all these beautiful women, Shaw once reportedly replied: "Should I have married ugly ones?"). He also reportedly had affairs with Betty Grable, Lena Horne, Joan Crawford, and Judy Garland.

Shaw was one of the first white bandleaders to employ African-American musicians—singer Billie Holiday, trumpeters Oran "Hot Lips" Page and Roy Eldridge, and (briefly) drummer Zutty Singleton—in an era of intense racial prejudice. Like the late Norman Granz, jazz impresario and record producer, Shaw fought Jim Crow discrimination in the worlds of jazz and swing. (In 1947, Shaw, along with Tommy Dorsey, Count Basie, Nat King Cole, Coleman Hawkins, and Buddy Rich, signed a proposal, drafted by Granz, which pledged jazz musicians not to perform to segregated audiences).

A musician of remarkable talent and ability, Shaw has not played the clarinet (in public or in private) for over forty years. But in the 1980s—largely due to the urging of the late Willard Alexander—he agreed to the re-formation of the Artie Shaw Orchestra, under the direction of clarinetist Dick Johnson.

The subject of Brigitte Berman's excellent film biography *Time Is All You've Got* (1984), which won an Academy Award for best documentary film, Shaw has more recently been interviewed by Fred Hall on station KKSB in California, in a six-hour "Tribute to Artie Shaw." The only detailed examination of Shaw's career is Edmund L. Blandford's privately published *Artie Shaw: A Bio-Discography* (1973). Despite its extensive use of articles and interviews which appeared in *Down Beat* and *Metronome* magazines, and a comprehensive listing of Shaw's recordings as a sideman and leader from 1931–1954, Blandford's book is shoddily presented, poorly written, and excessively adulatory. There is little sustained attempt to place Shaw's musical career in its historical and/or musical context, and no attention is given to his literary output.

The present study—reflecting a growing academic and popular interest in jazz and its derivatives—offers a narrative account and analytical assessment of the achievements and concerns of a major figure in American popular music. More specifically, it treats Shaw's formative years, his searches for a musical and personal identity, literary endeavors, questionings of the American myth of success, and engagement with political and racial issues. It also utilizes oral testimonies and the statements of Shaw's admirers and detractors.

At the beginning of the twenty-first century, Artie Shaw is one of the last great survivors of the Swing Era—that period in America's history when jazz-inflected music, performed by large orchestras and small groups reached new levels of precision, perfection, and polyphony which, although they can never be satisfactorily recreated, can still be heard in their original (and sometimes "enhanced") glory on record, cassette, and compact disc. Shaw himself has taken advantage of and invested in the new technology. His Web site (www.artieshaw.com) includes a third-person capsule autobiography that eschews false modesty and exudes staggering self-esteem. A few examples will illustrate the point:

> He made his first public appearance as a leader in 1936, in a Swing Concert (history's first) held at Broadway's Imperial Theater. This proved to be a major turning point in his career, and would in fact ultimately have a significant impact on the future of American Big Band jazz.

> Superstardom turned out to be a status that Shaw (a compulsive perfectionist) found totally uncongenial.

> Shaw is regarded by many as the finest and most innovative of all jazz clarinetists, a leader of several of the greatest musical aggregations ever assembled, and one of the most adventurous and accomplished figures in American music.

> As Shaw goes on into his nineties, he has also developed a crusty humor, as evidenced by an epitaph for himself he wrote for Who's Who in America a few years ago at the request of the editors: "He did the best he could with the material at hand."

Critic Gary Giddins suggests that "what is most paradoxical about Shaw is his resentment of celebrity obligations and his desire to sustain a celebrity-sized following." Perhaps too generously, Giddins concludes that it is "best take him at his word when he insists that he was temperamentally unsuited to the whole star-making apparatus."[1]

Every author of a "scholarly" text owes debts of gratitude to friends, colleagues, and librarians. My special thanks go to Midge Hayes, Artie Shaw's former assistant and companion, for her invaluable help in providing me with records, tapes, and photographs, but above all for her enthusiastic encouragement and pertinent observations—all of which helped to bring this book to fruition. I hope that it meets with her approval. Dan Morgenstern and the staff at the Institute of Jazz Studies, Rutgers University, Newark, New Jersey (the most relaxed and relaxing of archives) made my initial researches as rewarding as they were enjoyable. Artie Shaw's two collections of short stories (discussed in chapter 4) were read and "deconstructed" by my colleague (and fellow jazz enthusiast) John Mowat, Lecturer in American Literature at the University of Hull, who then generously shared his insights with me. I also acknowledge my indebtedness to the writings of Edmund L. Blandford, Leonard Feather, George T. Simon, Gunther Schuller, Vladimir Simosko, Alyn Shipton, Richard M. Sudhalter, and Robert Lewis Taylor for much of the information presented here. I must thank my good friend and collaborator Richard Palmer, for his close reading of and trenchant comments on several drafts of *Non-Stop Flight*. Thanks also to Alyn Shipton, who reviewed the first edition of this book on his *Jazz Notes* programme (BBC Radio 3) and then allowed and encouraged me to refine and reconsider my assessment of Artie Shaw—the man and his music.

John White
North Ferriby
East Yorkshire

1 March 2003

NOTE

1. Gary Giddins, *Visions of Jazz: The First Century* (New York and Oxford: Oxford University Press, 1998), 205–06.

The new *Swing* icon

Perspectives on Swing

You could buy Benny Goodman records until 1938, and then somebody must have realized he was Jewish. After that you could buy Artie Shaw records because they did not know his real name was Arshawsky.

Carlo Bohlander [German jazz historian]

Most jazz historians and critics agree that the Swing Era in America was launched with the sensational success of the Benny Goodman orchestra's engagement at the Palomar Ballroom in Los Angeles in 1935, at the end of its less-than-successful transcontinental tour. The young dancers at the Palomar had listened to Goodman's *Let's Dance* hour-long broadcasts for the National Biscuit Company (at a time when their East Coast counterparts were safely in bed), purchased his recordings of *Blue Skies* and *Sometimes I'm Happy*, and were simply waiting the arrival in person of their hero and his sidemen. By 1936 Goodman had been hailed by publicists—unaware of or indifferent to the fact that many of his arrangements like *King Porter Stomp* were by the African-American bandleader Fletcher Henderson—as "The King of Swing."[1] The American critic Barry Ulanov writes that "in the middle and late thirties, swing lost its standing as a verb and was elevated to the stature of a noun and a category. Jazz was dead, long live swing." Yet as the late Leonard Feather, British-born jazz enthusiast and promoter, believed:

If the swing era was born with the thunderous success of the Goodman band in California in the fall of 1935, it can be said to have enjoyed its baptism at the Imperial Theater in New York on Sunday evening, May 24, 1936, when Joe Helbock, the manager of the Onyx Club, decided to bring respectability to the trend by presenting the first official "Swing Music Concert." Though Goodman and Duke Ellington were absent, the personnel at the Imperial that night constituted to a large extent a *Who's Who* of the swing era. The participants included Bob Crosby, fronting the big orchestra that pioneered in the attempt to turn Dixieland jazz into a vehicle for a full-sized band; Tommy Dorsey, with a so-called "Clambake Seven" contingent from the new big band he had formed on breaking up with his brother Jimmy; violinist Stuff Smith, xylophonist Red Norvo and trumpeter Bunny Berigan with their swing sextets; Glen Gray's Casa Loma orchestra, and groups from the bands of Paul Whiteman and Louis Armstrong.

But the surprise of the evening came from an unexpected quarter and a relatively unknown performer.

> Perhaps the least impressive item on the printed programme announced the appearance of "Arthur Shaw's String Ensemble." Shaw, then a radio station musician and almost unknown to jazz fans, had decided to make a revolutionary move by backing his jazz clarinet with a string quartet. To the astonishment of Helbock, of the audience and above all of Shaw him-

self, the group's performance of Artie's *Interlude in B Flat* was the hit of the evening. Within a few months of his unexpected triumph at the Imperial Theater, Artie Shaw created the first major schism in the swing field. Benny Goodman, after a year of unchallenged supremacy, had a rival. The rivalry became more intense when Shaw, after abandoning his first jazz-with-strings orchestra, formed a band with the conventional brass-reeds-and rhythm constitution.[2]

During the "Swing Era" in America—roughly the period from 1935 to 1945—big-band music, already pioneered by the African-American aggregations of Don Redman and Fletcher Henderson, was popularized (and sometimes diluted) by the white orchestras of Tommy and Jimmy Dorsey, Benny Goodman, Glenn Miller, Charlie Barnet, Gene Krupa, and Harry James. Individually and collectively, these big-band leaders achieved an enormous following at home and abroad, and "jazz" and "swing" became synonymous terms for American popular music, heard on records, radio, and jukeboxes. Following the repeal of Prohibition in 1933, the exciting new music was heard in clubs and dance halls again permitted to sell alcohol.[3] According to one estimate, by 1940 there were close to two hundred orchestras, offering stylized and immediately identifiable forms of swing. Every swing orchestra had its complement of ardent and sometimes hysterical admirers—forerunners of today's rock and pop groupies—who possessed an awesome knowledge of their personnel, arrangers, recordings, and off-the-stand activities. As one contemporary observer recorded:

Among many of the jitterbugs—particularly among many of the boys and girls—the appreciation of the new music was largely vertebral. A good swing band smashing away at full speed, with the trumpeters and clarinetists rising in turn under the spotlight to embroider the theme with their several furious improvisations and the drummers going into long-drawn-out rhythmical frenzies, could reduce its less inhibited auditors to sheer emotional vibration, punctuated by howls of rapture.'[4]

Swing orchestras also had their theme tunes. Among the most famous were *One O'Clock Jump* (Count Basie), *Let's Dance* and *Goodbye* (Benny Goodman), *Blue Flame* (Woody Herman), *I'm Getting Sentimental Over You* (Tommy Dorsey), *Moonlight Serenade* (Glenn Miller), *Cherokee* (Charlie Barnet), *Chant of the Weed* (Don Redman), *Snowfall* (Claude Thornhill), *Deep Forest* (Earl Hines), and *Nightmare* (Artie Shaw). Jazz writer Nat Hentoff recalls:

> My own introduction to the jazz life began with a record of Artie Shaw's *Nightmare*. I came from a home where any overt expression of emotion was calculated and measured lest it roar out of control. Standing in a record store one afternoon, however, I shocked myself by yelling in pleasure at the first bars of *Nightmare*.

He adds that after Shaw "I went to Duke Ellington, Louis Armstrong, Fats Waller, blues singer Peetie Wheatstraw and I was hooked."[5]

For all swing orchestras, the role of *arrangers* was vital—since swing music was, in effect, "arranged improvisation." They worked closely with their respective leaders (some of whom were notable arrangers in their own right) and it was the arranger who helped swing bands to achieve their distinctive sound and identity. Notable arrangers of the swing era included Billy Strayhorn (Duke Ellington), Jerry Gray (Artie Shaw and Glenn Miller), Ray Conniff, Buster Harding and Johnny Mandel (Artie Shaw), and Eddie Sauter (Benny Goodman and Artie Shaw).

Radio stations like WNEW in New York and KFWB in Los Angeles, with their "Make Believe Ballrooms," featured programs by swing bands, many of which were sponsored—in those unenlightened and litigation-free times—by cigarette companies. Benny Goodman and Bob Crosby were presented by Camel; Glenn Miller and Harry James by Chesterfield; Larry Clinton, Woody Herman, and Artie Shaw by Old Gold and Tommy Dorsey by Raleigh-Kool. Established swing orchestras were also broadcast by "remotes"—usually late at night—from the hotels, restaurants, and theaters where they were appearing. Venues such as the Sherman Hotel (Chicago), Frank Dailey's Meadowbrook Inn (Cedar Grove, New Jersey), the Palomar Ballroom (Los Angeles), and Glen Island Casino (New Rochelle, New York) afforded the swing orchestras valuable exposure, publicity, and earnings.

> Working almost as if by plan, the national broadcasters piped hotel music to hundreds of thousands of people who would then flock to dance halls and theaters to hear these same bands on tour, after which the broadcasters could sell the bands to sponsors who wished their products to be associated with these by now "name bands."[6]

George T. Simon, veteran chronicler of the big bands, observes that remote broadcasts also meant that "bands would accept low wages for engagements in spots with radio outlets," often for weeks at a time and losing money, but hoping to gain enough national recognition through air time so "that when they finally did go out on one-nighters and theater tours, they could demand and get more money."[7]

In the 1930s and early 40s, the big radio networks also competed to present the top-name swing orchestras to their listeners. In 1939, the National Broadcasting Company (NBC) carried forty-nine name bands over its two networks (the Red and the Blue) including those of Charlie Barnet, Count Basie, the Dorsey Brothers, Gene Krupa, Glenn Miller, and Artie Shaw. The Columbia Broadcasting System (CBS) offered Benny Goodman, Jack Teagarden, and Cab Calloway, among its much smaller roster of swing bands.

The swing phenomenon was also very much a part of the American commercial entertainment business. David W. Stowe suggests plausibly that:

> The utopian impulses that big-band jazz seemed to embody and express—freedom, individualism, ethnic inclusiveness, democratic participation—were ones that inevitably put the music and its practitioners into conflict with the tendency of the swing industry toward consolidation, vertical integration, and homogenization. If swing was the popular music of most of the 1930s and 1940s, and therefore the first music to be acted upon by a new kind of culture industry, it was a particular kind of popular music, one that marked the media through which it gained its mass appeal.[8]

Swing orchestras were under the control of managers and agents, who often exploited as much as they promoted their clients.

Scott DeVeaux has remarked pertinently that the swing phenomenon was generated by

> a *system* of economic interdependence in which individual
> musicians played clearly defined roles. In the Swing Era, the
> integration of dance music with other forms of mass-market
> entertainment was carried out on a scale never seen before.
> New media—radio, recordings, film—began to tie the vast
> American continent together into networks of production and
> dissemination controlled from New York and Los Angeles.
> Each step brought new efficiencies that increased the poten-
> tial for profit, while requiring the individual to yield more and
> more autonomy to the system [which] with its booking agen-
> cies, radio broadcasts, and record contracts, was pervasive and
> all-inclusive. To exist outside of it was either an admission of
> incompetence or an act of rebellion.[9]

Booking agencies like the General Artists Corporation
(GAC)—formed by Tommy Rockwell and Francis (Corky)
O'Keefe—promoted the bands of Bob Crosby, Jimmy Dorsey,
Woody Herman, Glenn Miller, and Artie Shaw. The Music Corporation of America (MCA)—founded by Jules C. Stein—signed
up Shaw's future rival Benny Goodman at the start of his career,
and the Count Basie Orchestra after its arrival in New York from
Kansas City in 1936. Moreover, bandleaders were constantly im-
portuned by publishers' representatives—"song-pluggers"—to
get particular tunes played over the air. Trombonist Tommy
Dorsey, like other band leaders, was highly critical of these
salesmen.

> They come in and instead of a direct "Here's a tune that I
> think will be good for the band; please look it over," they try

hard as hell to be subtle, put their arms around me, shake my one hand with two of theirs—all in an attempt to make me believe that they love me and that I'm really one helluva wonderful guy. But I know exactly what they are driving at and that at any minute they're going to drive in for the kill with the usual stuff about the most "terrific tune" of the year.[10]

In 1941, when the networks rejected the demand of the American Society of Authors, Composers and Publishers (ASCAP) that they should increase payment for performing the work of its members, many orchestras were forced to play swing versions of old standards like *London Bridge is Falling Down*, *Comin' Through the Rye*, *Loch Lomond*, and *My Old Kentucky Home* that were out of copyright. There were also swing versions of such "classical" pieces as Mendelssohn's *Spring Song* and Johann Strauss's *The Blue Danube*—both of which were performed by Tommy Dorsey in 1937. Musical purists denounced such depredations and demanded that they be banned from the airwaves. One such protest concerned Benny Goodman's recording of *Bach Goes to Town* (1938), composed by Alec Templeton and arranged by Henry Brant. The president of the Bach Society of Newark, New Jersey, protested to the Federal Communications Commission (FCC), and suggested that "any station that violates the canon of decency, by permitting the syncopation of the classics, particularly Bach's music, be penalized by having its licence suspended." The FCC declined to issue such a ruling, but did ask radio stations to exercise "a high degree of discrimination" in featuring such material.[11]

Swing performances, whatever their provenance—and perhaps not surprisingly—also met with a hostile reception from some quarters of the American press and self-appointed guardians of public taste. Krin Gabbard in his examination of [mis]representations of jazz in Hollywood movies, notes that "many white Americans embraced swing because it contained elements associated with African-American spontaneity, transgressiveness, and, most importantly, sexuality. These elements were clearly implied even when the music was played by an entirely white band."[12]

Many contemporary commentators perceived—as they also deplored—this connection. According to one pundit, "swing deals largely with eroticism—hence its restlessness and pain and gloom, its mad excitements and its profound despairs."[13] In 1938, Professor H. D. Gideonese of Columbia University, with a fine disregard for logic or contemporary political realities, informed four hundred Barnard College undergraduates that "swing is musical Hitlerism. There is a mass sense of letting one's self go." In the same year, the president of the Dancing Teacher's Business Association told its annual convention that in swing music, young people found "neurotic and erotic expressions of physical activity."[14] These and similar diatribes led Paul Eduard Miller to conclude in *Down Beat's Yearbook of Swing* (1939) that: "No other music, to my knowledge, has suffered so much violent criticism nor has been the subject of so many spurious attacks by both professional and non-professional reformers of the world's morals."[15]

Yet as Neil Leonard has ably demonstrated, by the late 1930s denigrations of swing were being countered by expressions of approval and understanding. In 1941, the director of the Radio Artist's Guild of America declared that "Benny Goodman has brought to popular music a virtuosity which many symphonic instrumentalists envy." Two years earlier, Mrs. Lilla Bell Pitts, vice-president of the Music Educators' National Conference, while not endorsing the preference of America's youth for swing music, urged her fellow educators to recognize its appeal, and endorsed Alec Templeton's verdict that "if Johann Sebastian Bach were alive today he and Benny Goodman would be the best of friends."[16]

Big bands and swing stars also appeared in Hollywood movies of the 1930s and 40s—which generally ranged from mediocre to abominable in quality and accuracy. Gene Krupa was featured in the Gary Cooper/Barbara Stanwyck comedy, *Ball of Fire*, directed by Howard Hawks (1941), in which he played *Drum Boogie*—switching from drumsticks to matchsticks in the final coda. *Las Vegas Nights*, directed by Ralph Murphy (1941), included the Tommy Dorsey Orchestra and an invisible string section. It was not all dross. The Benny Goodman Quartet and Orchestra made appearances that were both musically and visually satisfying in the Busby Berkeley musical *Hollywood Hotel* (1937).[17]

Most swing orchestras and small groups centered on their leaders and their respective instruments: Bunny Berigan, Ziggy Elman, and Harry James (trumpeters), Tommy Dorsey, Buddy Morrow, and Jack Teagarden (trombonists), Benny Goodman, Woody Herman, and Artie Shaw (clarinetists), Charlie Barnet, Jimmy Dorsey, and Sam Donahue (saxophonists), Duke Ellington, Count Basie, and Earl Hines (pianists), Gene Krupa and Chick Webb (drummers).

Swing bands, then, played versions of original and popular tunes, all of which were characterized by the "call-and-response" interplay between the brass and reed sections, unison choruses, a steady 4/4 rhythm (provided by the "rhythm section" of piano, bass, guitar, and drums), and improvised solos from featured instrumentalists. Some swing orchestras—notably those of Artie Shaw, Harry James, Glenn Miller, and Tommy Dorsey—featured string sections. From the late 1930s, resident and peripatetic vocalists came to be identified with the major leaders: Peggy Lee and Martha Tilton (Benny Goodman), Helen Forrest (Artie Shaw, Benny Goodman, and Harry James), Billie Holiday (Count Basie and Artie Shaw), Ella Fitzgerald (Chick Webb), Lena Horne (Charlie Barnet), and Frank Sinatra (Harry James and Tommy Dorsey).[18] Whatever their talents, swing-band vocalists provided "the most personal, the most literal and often the most communicative link between the bandstands and the dance floors, between stages and seats, and between recording and radio studios and the perennial 'unseen audiences.'"[19]

Explanations for the rise of swing are as varied as they are generally unsatisfactory. An editorial in *Metronome* magazine in 1938 asserted that swing "began to take hold in a national way" at about the same time as the United States began to emerge from the Great Depression and entered the era of Democratic president Franklin D. Roosevelt's New Deal, with its programs of economic recovery and reform. Other commentators related the rise of the swing era to the fall of the American (and world) economy. In this view, swing—and the social activities that it encouraged—offered those suffering from the continuing after-

math of the Depression entertainment, escape, romance, and ec-
stasy. More recently, Gunther Schuller has offered an amalgam
of these views—of swing as representing, in part, an antidote to
harsh economic realities, as signifying a "searching for deeper life
values and means of spiritual fulfilment rather than the pursuit
of material acquisition." It was also a commercial and creative
response to the more sanguine atmosphere generated by Roosevelt's vigorous and innovative political leadership.

> Despite the Depression—or perhaps because of it—the thir-
> ties were for many people a new beginning. For some minori-
> ties the period represented another small but significant step
> up the ladder of social and cultural integration and, for many
> blacks, opportunities in music—in jazz, that is—were to open
> new vistas of economic and social status. In the wake of the
> initiative begun in the Jazz Age, the 1920s, more black musi-
> cians saw jazz for the first time as a profession. And some, per-
> haps, even dared to see it as an art.[20]

David Stowe has suggested (not entirely convincingly) that
big-band swing, with its emphasis on regimented performances
in which soloists made their personal contributions to the collective whole, was analogous to "the notion of a co-operative com-
monwealth central to Franklin Roosevelt's vision of America."
Swing's exponents and their audiences reflected the Democratic
Party's constituency of organized labor, intellectuals, farmers,
and urban ethnic groups. Lewis Erenberg makes the insightful
observations that "swing was profoundly cosmopolitan, including
blacks, Jews, Italians, Poles, Irish and Protestants as leaders,
players, and singers." Charlie Barnet had rejected his privileged

and wealthy background to pursue the exciting jazz life; Artie Shaw, the former Arthur Arshawsky, sought fame and fortune in the music business as an "alternative to his parents' Jewish identity." African-American musicians hoped that swing music would provide them with both artistic and commercial opportunities. Fletcher Henderson, Don Redman, Duke Ellington, and Count Basie melded the African-American improvisatory tradition with a Eurocentric musical tradition.

But there is no entirely persuasive explanation for the rise and vogue of swing. As the historian and jazz enthusiast Edward Pessen concludes, "the growing popularity of swing music *correlated* with any number of social, political, economic, and intellectual trends of the late 1930s. That fact, however, proves nothing and offers no evidence that it was these trends that induced people to respond positively to what to them was a new kind of music or induced musicians to play it."[21]

Certainly the black orchestras of Jimmie Lunceford, Count Basie, Lionel Hampton, Earl Hines, Chick Webb, and Duke Ellington made their own—and generally superior—contributions to the swing years. They also had their white admirers. In his autobiography *Along This Way* (1933), James Weldon Johnson, the African-American novelist, songwriter and civil rights activist, observed the growing popularity of what he called "this lighter music" which "has been fused and then developed, chiefly by Jewish musicians," into a national popular idiom.

> It is to this music that America in general gives itself over in its leisure hours, when it is not engaged in the struggles imposed upon it by the exigencies of present-day American life.

At these times, the Negro drags his captors captive. On occasions, I have been amazed and amused watching white people
dancing to a Negro band in a Harlem cabaret; attempting to
throw off the crusts and layers of inhibitions laid on by sophisticated civilization; striving to yield to the feel and experience
of abandon; seeking to recapture a state of primitive joy in life
and living; trying to work their way back into that jungle which
was the original Garden of Eden; in a word, doing their best
to pass for colored.[22]

The world of swing, was "more racially and ethnically mixed
than any other arena of American life," and its ideology was both
"utopian" and "cosmopolitan." Despite racial discrimination in
the music industry, black bands, with the support and encouragement of such left-wing enthusiasts as John Hammond, now
"had the opportunity to aspire to national acclaim." As Scott De-
Veaux observes, although African-American musicians gained
only limited benefits from the New Deal, they made some prog-
ress. "Sceptical as they may have been of any opportunities offered by white society, they must have been tantalized by the
possibility for change." But in a period of intense racial discrimination, African-American musicians did not receive the exposure, facilities or public recognition accorded to their white
counterparts.[23] Yet as the British critic Stanley Dance perceived,
"the general preference of [the] white masses for jazz by white
musicians was never altogether the result of racial prejudice.
Translations, and indeed dilutions, were understandably more to
their taste."[24] African-American jazz artists were, however, ac-
knowledged by their fellow white musicians as sources of inspiration, who were to be emulated—if not actually offered
employment.[25]

Yet just what swing *was* remained a matter of conjecture and controversy, partly because as Ross Firestone has noted, the new form—however defined—"did not really involve any radical break in the jazz tradition." Unlike the "bop" or "bebop" revolution of the 1940s (or the "free jazz" revolution of the 1960s) swing was an *evolutionary* rather than a *revolutionary* development. Moreover, given the common identification of swing with large orchestras, there is a certain irony in the fact that it was small groups of musicians, playing "novelty" numbers, and fronted by such leaders as Louis Prima and Wingy Manone (both trumpeters) who initially popularized the new jazz style.[26] But as "swing" began to enjoy popular currency, leaders of large orchestras increasingly began to bill themselves as "swing" bands— possibly because the term lacked the racial and sexual connotations popularly associated with the word "jazz."[27]

During World War II, Artie Shaw's Navy Band, the Glenn Miller Army Air Force Band, other swing-inflected aggregations—and the "V-Discs" made by swing and jazz musicians expressly for the Armed Forces—did much to sustain American military morale. On the eve of World War II, *Time* magazine reported that to most Germans, the United States meant "skyscrapers, Clark Gable, and Artie Shaw." A German officer, captured by the advancing Americans in 1945, reportedly asked, "Do you have any Count Basie records?" As Gunther Schuller observes, "This special identity between a people and its music is perhaps the happiest and most significant aspect of the Swing Era, a quality impossible to recapture now, and, for those who did not actually experience it, difficult to savour in retrospect."[28] If the offerings of white swing orchestras eventually became sterile, mechanical, and meretricious, the classic performances by the bands of Charlie Barnet, Bunny Berigan, Tommy Dorsey, Harry James, Benny Goodman, and Artie Shaw were frequently rewarding and musically intelligent.

In their comprehensive analysis of jazz styles in New York City, Samuel Charters and Leonard Kunstadt suggest that given their "brilliant musicianship and complex arrangements," swing orchestras could have reached one of the highest levels of musical achievement that any popular dance music had ever achieved. But sadly (and increasingly) "for every imaginative and creative arrangement they played," there were "ten tedious accompaniments for the singing of the band's romantic crooner. For every exhilarating moment of swinging rhythm and drive there were ten of the most hackneyed dance music."[29]

In similar vein, Hsio Wen Shih has suggested that it was the *sameness* of swing orchestrations and performances that resulted in the demise of classic big-band swing.

> The increasing popularity of swing arrangements on the [Fletcher] Henderson model led to a general similarity of style in all the big bands. Goodman, Shaw, the Dorseys, Barnet, [Earl] Hines, [Cab] Calloway, and [Chick] Webb were all approaching the same standards of proficiency. By the early 1940s the gradual elimination of stylistic variations had killed big-band jazz. It was death by entropy.[30]

Yet Frederick Lewis Allen, a perceptive commentator on contemporary American culture and mores, was more impressed by the fact that even before the United States entered World War II, the great swing units had produced music that was often both subtle and complex, and required much more of its devotees than did the popular music of earlier decades.

> The true swing enthusiasts, who only collected records to the limit of their means and not only liked Artie Shaw's rendering of *Begin the Beguine* but knew precisely why they liked it, were receiving no mean musical education; and if Benny Goodman could turn readily from the playing of *Don't Be That Way* to the playing of Mozart, so could many of his hearers turn to the hearing of Mozart. It may not have been quite accidental that the craze for swing accompanied the sharpest gain in musical knowledge and musical taste that the American people had ever achieved.[31]

At the conclusion of a concert and lecture series at New York City's Town Hall in 1938, presented by Benny Goodman and John Erskine, president of the Julliard School of Music, the *New York Times* reported:

> The audience might have assembled to hear a programme of Bach, Beethoven and Brahms. For subscribers of a series that had presented serious lecture-recitals on lieder, the symphony, the string quartet and other sober manifestations of the musical art, the response to what was perhaps their first face-to-face experience in swing must have been altogether encouraging to friends of swing. The applause and cheers that followed Mr. Goodman's music left no doubt that the classics had not spoiled the audience forever for the delights of hot jazz or swing. Although occupants of the orchestra seats maintained a concert-going reserve, those in the balcony were not ashamed to sway their shoulders and paid no heed to restless feet.[32]

Swing was a participatory phenomenon. Its young audiences were not simply the passive recipients of commercially based musical products, but informed and dedicated collaborators in a musical and cultural revolution. Transcending lines of class and race, by the mid-1930s swing and its devotees exemplified American popular culture. In the era of the New Deal, with its appeal to the nation's diverse ethnic groups, swing—as James Weldon Johnson perceived—reflected the impact of European immigrant cultures on established American White Anglo-Saxon Protestant norms. In the 1930s, the fusion of syncretic Euro-American musical forms with a vibrant African-American tradition produced the exotic hybrid that was designated "swing." It was, therefore, wholly appropriate that two of the greatest exemplars of the Swing Era—Artie Shaw and Benny Goodman—emerged from the East-European Jewish enclaves in the urban and industrialized America of the 1900s.

NOTES

1. Barry Ulanov, *Duke Ellington* (London: Musicians Press, 1947). "There was no difference between the two kinds of music but distinctions were being made. Swing meant arranged big-band jazz to the majority of fans and musicians, who used it to denote and connote the new music." 166.

2. Leonard Feather, *The Encylopedia of Jazz* (New York: Bonanza Books, 1960), 28. The Imperial Theatre "Swing Music Concert" was soon followed by other presentations—most notably, Benny Goodman's sensational appearance with his orchestra and stars from the Duke Ellington and Count Basie bands at Carnegie Hall on January 16, 1938, and record producer John Hammond's two "Spirituals to Swing" con-

certs (supported by the Socialist paper *New Masses*), also at Carnegie Hall in 1938/39.

3. In 1933 there were 25,000 jukeboxes in the United States; by 1939, the number had risen to 300,000. Record sales of jazz and swing music showed a similar increase. Six million records were sold in 1933; by 1938, sales had reached over 33 million.

4. Frederick Lewis Allen, *Since Yesterday* (New York: Bantam Books, 1961), 214.

5. Nat Hentoff, *The Jazz Life* (London: Peter Davies, 1962), 9.

6. Broadcasters made "remotes" by running wires to these venues, where transmitters picked up the live musical performances and broadcast them over the radio. "Places featuring live music gladly permitted remote broadcasting of the programs, for it meant free advertising, often on a national scale, and musicians in search of exposure welcomed the opportunity to get their music broadcast at no charge to themselves." James P. Kraft, *Stage to Studio: Musicians and the Sound Revolution, 1890–1950* (Baltimore and London: The Johns Hopkins University Press, 1996), 68. Leroy Ostransky, *The Anatomy of Jazz* (Seattle: University of Washington Press, 1960), 224.

7. George T. Simon, *The Big Bands* (New York: Macmillan, 1971), 58. "The big swing bands entered into a symbiotic relationship with the radio stations. For radio, the bands playing in the restaurants and dance halls were a golden source of free programming; for the bands, radio was an equally golden fountain of free publicity." James Lincoln Collier, *The Making of Jazz: A Comprehensive History* (London: Macmillan, 1981), 263.

8. David W. Stowe, *Swing Changes: Big-Band Jazz in New Deal America* (Cambridge, Mass. and London: Harvard University Press, 1994), 100. Erenberg suggests that in accounting for the rise of swing, historians have exaggerated the influence of commercial dissemination and considerations and the privileged position of white orchestras since the "paradigms of commercialism and the culture hegemony offer little insight into the music's appeal to a mass youth audience." Lewis A. Erenberg *Swinging the Dream: Big Band Jazz and the Rebirth of American Culture* (Chicago and London: University of Chicago Press, 1998), xii.

9. *The Birth of Bebop: A Social and Musical History* (Berkeley, Los Angeles and London: University of California Press, 1997), 118–19.

10. Simon, *The Big Bands*, 60–61.

11. Ross Firestone, *Swing, Swing, Swing: The Life and Times of Benny Goodman* (London: Hodder and Stoughton, 1993), 243.

12. Krin Gabbard, *Jammin' at the Margins: Jazz and the American Cinema*, (Chicago and London: University of Chicago Press, 1996), 27.

13. Barry Edward, "This Mad Thing Called Swing!" *Chicago Sunday Tribune*, December 11, 1938.

14. Neil Leonard, *Jazz and the White Americans: The Acceptance of a New Art Form* (Chicago: University of Chigago Press, 1963), 153. Lawrence Levine's comment on the detractors and champions of jazz in the 1920s applies equally to the controversy over swing in the 1930s. "Jazz was often praised for possessing precisely those characteristics that made it anathema to those who condemned it: it was praised and criticized for being innovative and breaking with tradition. It was praised and criticized for breaking out of the tight circle of obeisance to Eurocentric cultural forms and giving expression to indigenous American attitudes articulated through indigenous American creative structures. It was, in short, praised and criticized for being almost completely out of phase with the period's concept of Culture." "Jazz and American Culture," in Levine, *The Unpredictable Past: Explorations in American Cultural History* (New York and Oxford: Oxford University Press, 1993), 180–81.

15. *Swing, Swing, Swing*, 242.

16. *Jazz and the White Americans*, 146; 151. The leading exponents of white swing also looked respectable. "The celebrity bandleaders with whom the American public associated swing in the late 1930s—Goodman, Dorsey, Shaw, Miller—embodied in their persons the visual style of the musical fad. [They] were impeccably groomed, not surprisingly, but their appearances also suggested moderation and sobriety. Goodman was once described as looking like a high school science teacher." Stowe, *Swing Changes*, 45.

17. Hollywood's presentations of jazz musicians has been ably charted by David Meeker in *Jazz in the Movies: A Guide to Jazz Musicians*

1917–1977 (London: Talisman Books, 1977). See also: Gabbard, *Jammin' at the Margins*. Gabbard observes that: "psychoanalytic and structuralist film theorists have pointed out [that] musical numbers bring the film's story to an abrupt halt. [But] since narrative is indisputably what most audiences crave, then a film about jazz [or swing] or a film with jazz cannot dwell on the music for too long. The music gets shoved aside to make way for the action, or worse, the music continues, barely audible in the background while the actors talk. Still worse, performances by some of the most revered jazz artists are the least likely to appear on film. For many years black artists were simply left out or confined to short performance scenes that could be excised by nervous exhibitors." 6.

Unaware (perhaps mercifully) of structuralist film theory, a *Down Beat* writer observed in 1941: "Hollywood is suffering from a frustration complex. It is excruciatingly aware of the box-office value of dance orchestras, but it hasn't the faintest idea of just what to do about it. No one has, as yet, come up with a sure-fire formula for the use of dance bands in pictures—a formula, which by Hollywood tradition, must eliminate the necessity for imagination and inspiration." Quoted in David W. Stowe, *Swing Changes*, 136.

18. Frank Sinatra often commented that as an apprentice vocalist he had learned a lot by simply sitting on the bandstand with Tommy Dorsey and watching his breath-control technique as he played the trombone.

19. Simon, *The Big Bands*, 33.

20. Schuller, *The Swing Era: The Development of Jazz, 1930–1945* (New York and Oxford: Oxford University Press, 1985), 5.

21. Lewis A. Erenberg, "Things to Come: Swing Bands, Bebop, and the Rise of the Postwar Jazz Scene," in Larry May, ed., *Recasting America: Culture and Politics in the Age of the Cold War* (Chicago and London: University of Chicago Press, 1989), 277–8. Edward Pessen, "The Kingdom of Swing: New York City in the Late 1930s," *New York History*, LXXX (July 1989), 308.

22. *Along This Way: The Autobiography of James Weldon Johnson* (London: Penguin Books, 1990), 328.

23. *Swinging the Dream*, 250; *The Birth of Bebop*, 119. Schuller notes that "when the 'swing' styles reigned supreme, it was the swing music of Goodman, Miller, and Shaw, not Ellington and [Jimmie] Lunceford, that became the popular music of the land." *The Swing Era*, 199.

24. Stanley Dance, *The World of Swing* (New York: Charles Scribner's Sons, 1974), 10.

25. The extent and degree of color blindness among white bandleaders and swing entrepreneurs should not be exaggerated. Gabbard observes that "Popular understanding of jazz among whites began to allow for a greater black presence in the 1930s. Artie Shaw, John Hammond, and Benny Goodman deserve credit for their mixed bands of that decade. Their first steps in this direction, however, were tentative: Hammond saw to it that Billie Holiday did not appear in public with the white musicians with whom she recorded in the mid-thirties; when Goodman first brought Teddy Wilson and later Lionel Hampton on stage, he and Gene Krupa performed with them while his [Goodman's] all-white orchestra was offstage; and a year passed after Goodman's first recordings with blacks before he would perform with them in public." *Jammin' at the Margins*, 19.

26. *Swing, Swing, Swing*, 156–7. Firestone points out that one song in particular—*The Music Goes 'Round and 'Round*—recorded by trumpeter Eddie Farley and trombonist Mike Riley for the Decca label in September, 1935, introduced an embryonic form of "swing" to a nationwide audience. An immediate success—it sold over a hundred thousand copies—"the song attracted such huge crowds to the Onyx [Club] where Riley and Farley now led their own group, that there was hardly any room for the real jazz fans. And it helped make the kind of music becoming known as swing the latest national fad." 156.

27. On the day that Benny Goodman opened his engagement at the Congress Hotel in Chicago (November 6, 1935), "*Variety* introduced a new weekly column by Abel Green titled 'Swing Stuff,' a sure sign that the word had by now entered the show business mainstream and that the music referred to was beginning to register a significant commercial aspect." *Ibid*. 155. Scott DeVeaux relates that shortly after the onset of

"the initial swing craze, dance orchestras generated nearly $100 million annually, employing some thirty to forty thousand musicians, as well as another eight thousand managers, promoters, and other support personnel." *The Birth of Bebop*, 127.

28. *The Swing Era*, 4.

29. *Jazz: A History of the New York Scene*, 241. Jazz historian and critic Martin Williams delivered very much the same verdict. "The big swing bands flourished roughly from the mid-1930s through the late 1940s, and by the early 1950s there were only a handful of survivors. Since we Americans are very fond of interpreting events in our national life in terms of economics, we are apt to say that the bands disappeared because the 'business' could no longer support them. But that is only another way of saying that large numbers of people no longer wanted to dance to their music, listen to their music, or buy their recordings. However, there was a valid artistic reason why the bands should not have survived. By the end of the 1940s their work was largely done— almost all their ideas had been thoroughly explored, thoroughly imitated and popularized, and only the greatest or most individual of them—Ellington being the supreme example—had pressing reasons to survive." *Jazz Heritage* (New York and Oxford: Oxford University Press, 1985), 31–2.

30. Hsio Wen Shih, "The Spread of Jazz and the Big Bands," in *Jazz*, edited by Nat Hentoff and Albert McCarthy (New York: Rinehart and Co., 1959), 186–7.

31. Frederick Lewis Allen, *Since Yesterday*, 215.

32. *Jazz and the White Americans*, 150.

Shaw and Billie Holiday, Boston, 1938
(attrib. Bob Inman)

Interlude in B Flat:
The Search for Identity

I don't dabble in anything; I get involved in whatever I do.

Artie Shaw

If you have a conversation with Artie Shaw and take a breath,
you lose your turn for about fifty minutes.

Mel Tormé

In 1914, over 1,400,000 Jews lived in New York City, where they were heavily concentrated in the Lower East Side, an area of little more than a square mile, extending from the Bowery almost to the East River, and from 14th Street to the Brooklyn Bridge. British novelist Arnold Bennett, on an American visit in 1912, said that on Rivington Street "the architecture seemed to sweat humanity at every window and door." Jewish immigrants from Russia, Romania, and Austria-Hungary inhabited five and six-storey "dumb-bell" tenements with dark rooms, shared toilets, and a cold-water tap typically supplying two apartments of four rooms at each end of the landing. Yiddish was the lingua franca of the Lower East Side, and its residents, many of whom were boarders, often sharing beds on a shift basis, were most commonly engaged in the manufacture of ready-made clothing for the garment trade.

Jacob Riis, a Danish-born police reporter and reform-minded journalist, observed in his celebrated study *How the Other Half Lives* (1890):

> The homes of the Hebrew quarter are its workshops also. You are made fully aware of it before you have travelled the length of a single block in any of these East Side streets, by the whirr of a thousand sewing machines, worked at high pressure from earliest dawn until mind and muscle give out together. It is not unusual to find a dozen persons—men, women and children—at work in a single room.[1]

In 1899, New York State adopted legislation governing tenement work, with a system of licensing and inspection to ensure minimum standards of ventilation and hygiene—the result of which was to drive workers out of the tenements and into factories. In September 1909, the Jewish-led Ladies' Garment Workers' Union and the Amalgamated Clothing Workers of America staged a successful strike in protest against working conditions, lasting until February 1910, and resulting in union recognition and wage increases. Another strike in the summer of 1910 called for a 48-hour week, the end of "sweatshop" conditions and union recognition of the cloak-makers' industry. It ended in victory, but on March 26, 1911, a fire broke out in the factory of the Triangle Waist Company, off Washington Place, in which 146 lives—mostly women and girls—were lost. Yet despite its crowded living and working conditions, the Lower East Side had low rates of death and disease—a phenomenon ascribed by health officials to the high standards of personal hygiene and the strict dietary laws required by the Jewish religion.

Sarah Strauss, a Jewish immigrant from Austria, and Harry Arshawsky, a Russian Jew, met and married in New York City, and their only son, Arthur Jacob Arshawsky, was born there on May 23, 1910. Nearly eight hundred miles away, and one year earlier, on May 30, 1909, Dora Goodman had given birth to her ninth child, Benjamin David, on Chicago's West Side. Her husband, David, was, like his wife, a Jewish immigrant from Poland, and worked in a clothing factory. Thirty years later, their son related:

> Pop was a tailor. He didn't have his own place but he worked in a factory, when there was work. At a time when I begin to remember things more clearly (about 1919, when I was nine years old), we were living on Francisco Avenue. It was one of those old three-storey brick houses they have all over the West Side in Chicago, with dark stairways, small rooms, not much light. This was a pretty hopeless neighbourhood, the Ghetto of Chicago that corresponded to the East Side in New York.[2]

Social reformer Jane Addams's 1910 description of Chicago's immigrant slums confirms the young Benny Goodman's memories:

> The streets are inexpressibly dirty, the number of schools inadequate, sanitary legislation unenforced, the street lighting bad, the paving miserable and altogether lacking in the alleys and smaller streets, the stables foul beyond description. Hundreds of houses are unconnected with the street sewer. The older

and richer inhabitants seem anxious to move away as rapidly as they can afford it.[3]

A similar pattern of immigrant aspiration operated on the East Coast. Artie Shaw (the former Arthur Arshawsky) recalled that his parents "were in the dressmaking business, doing their work on sewing machines in their basement apartment on Second Street, on the Lower East Side." When Shaw was seven years old, the family business became bankrupt, and the Arshawskys moved to a house on York Street, in New Haven, Connecticut (now part of Yale University campus), and resumed their dressmaking enterprise. The young Shaw, already an avid reader of such classics as *Kidnapped* and *Huckleberry Finn*, attended Dwight Street School in New Haven, where he quickly became aware of the anti-Semitism of his fellow pupils. Nicknamed "Columbus Arshawsky," he was told that "we don't want no goddam Christ-killers saying the Lord's prayer around here. Keep your dirty sheeny nose out of other people's prayers." The recipient of this unsolicited advice later reflected: "I now realize that it is practically impossible for any Jewish kid to grow up in the average American town—meaning a more or less predominantly Anglo-Saxon, Protestant community such as New Haven is now and was then—without becoming aware of the fact that he is some curious kind of alien."[4]

Although the young Arthur Arshawsky—a shy and introspective child—resisted the piano lessons imposed by his mother, he took up the ukulele and was a regular patron of Poli's Palace Theatre on Church Street in New Haven, a venue for vaudeville acts. On one occasion, he was profoundly impressed by a young performer in a vivid striped blazer who played a song called *Dreamy Melody* on a C-melody saxophone. Determined to acquire such an imposing instrument, Shaw (now aged 13) worked for the summer at Gorn's Delicatessen at a salary of four dollars a week, bought a C-melody saxophone—"my key to the golden kingdom"—from Wrozina's Music Shop, and practised for up to eight hours a day. Burton Peretti suggests plausibly that given his experiences of anti-Semitism in New Haven, Shaw's decision to become a musician owed less to musical inspiration than to a

> general ethnic passion to overcome marginality and to assimilate to what each immigrant's child perceived as being 'America.' In this respect he seems more intensely alienated than the more optimistically adventurous white players of Chicago [but] resembled them in that the 'America' he sought was not suburbia, but the urban jazz world.

Lewis Erenberg believes that Shaw "sought big-band success as an escape from both his parents' Jewish identity and the narrow bigotry and anti-Semitism of Christian America," and notes that he "was eager to play black-inspired music because he saw the blacks as the only group in the industrial age that still retained a sense of humanity and community."[5]

Unhappy with his marriage, Shaw's father left the family and went to California, and the aspiring saxophonist drew closer to his mother. At a neighborhood weekly amateur night in 1924, Shaw—dressed to his acute embarrassment in a Knickerbocker suit—won the first prize of five dollars for his rendition of *Charlie My Boy*. Determined to become a professional musician, he promptly purchased a record by saxophonist Rudy Wiedoeft, acquired an alto saxophone (which is tuned in E-flat), and began to wrestle with his new instrument—with little success and at the cost of sore lips and bleeding gums. But together with his friend Gene Beecher Jr., who played banjo, Shaw continued to perform at amateur nights, and then joined with three other youths (on piano, violin, and drums) to form the Peter Pan Novelty Orchestra, which played at local events, with the members taking turns to act as leader.

Shaw remembered that "although I had learned something about playing my instrument and had begun to develop a fair degree of improvisational skill, no one had bothered to inform me that I should also try to learn something about sight-reading."[6] Auditioned by Johnny Cavallaro, leader of a New Haven dance band that included trumpeter Charlie Spivak, Shaw confessed that he could not read music, and asked Cavallaro to hold the job open for him.

> A young saxophone player approached me and told me his greatest ambition was to play in my band. It was Art Shaw. I tried him out with my band and although I could see he had plenty of talent and a fair tone, he just missed coming up to the standard I required. I told him to go home, take a few more lessons and come back and see me in six months. He did and I put him in the band.[7]

Tenor saxophonist and vocalist Tony Pastor—later to join Shaw's first permanent orchestra in 1935—remembered his friendship with the aspiring musician in New Haven when: "Artie used to hang around with the John Cavallaro band in which I was playing and he'd carry my horn down to the railroad station for me. You see, I could play a whole tonal scale in those days, and I guess Artie must have thought I was a genius."[8]

In 1924, aged fourteen, Shaw left high school in his sophomore year, changed his name to Shaw (over his mother's initial objections, although she also later adopted the surname), and became a professional musician, playing alto saxophone with Cavallaro at the Cinderella Ballroom and the fraternity houses of Wesleyan University. Some sixty years later, Shaw reflected that when he began playing professionally, there were two types of popular music—"sweet" and "hot"—the latter form exemplified by pianist/leader Jean Goldkette.

> But we didn't call it jazz. We called it playing a "hot chorus." I would get up and play what we now call jazz. Basically, that was a sop to the musicians to get through the evening. You'd get bored to death playing *Mary Lou* all night. You'd go crazy. So you would finally say, "Hey, play a hot chorus song," so the guy would take the chords and improvise. That became interesting. It made the evening go better.[9]

Shaw also played "sweet" and "hot" music with other local outfits, including Eddie Wittstein's Society Orchestra and Lee Laden's band, which featured Rudy Vallee, a saxophonist and engaging crooner who was later to receive international fame. Reminiscing about this period, Shaw cited his musical influences as two white musicians: the C-melody saxophonist Frank Trumbauer, and cornetist Bix Beiderbecke—"Trumbauer for dexterity, but Bix musically."[10]

During an appearance of the Cavallaro band at Bantam Lake, a summer resort in Connecticut, Shaw had his first en-

counter with alcohol, and was fired after appearing on the bandstand dressed only in his swimming trunks. Back in New Haven,
he joined a short-lived local band called the Kentuckians which
(ironically), left him stranded in Lexington, Kentucky. He then
rejoined Cavallaro, who had engagements in Florida, and demanded that his re-hired sideman learn to play the clarinet.
Shaw discovered that the instrument, which was to bring him
fame and fortune, was extremely difficult to master. On a clarinet, the fingering is different from that of a saxophone and every
octave change involves several keys. Cavallaro was unimpressed
with Shaw's performances on his new instrument, and he was
again dropped when the band returned to New Haven.

While he was playing alto at New Haven's Olympia Theatre,
Shaw, with the help of drummer Chuck Cantor, obtained a job
with Cantor's brother, Joe, who was playing with his "Far East
Orchestra" at a Chinese restaurant on Euclid Avenue in Cleveland, Ohio. With his mother, Shaw moved to Cleveland, and he
began to arrange tunes for the Cantor band, and later transferred
to another Cleveland band, led by violinist Austin Wylie at the
Golden Pheasant Chinese Restaurant. Despite the support of his
mother, who insisted that he always dressed appropriately, Shaw
found the three daily sessions at Chinese dinner-and-dance restaurants boring and gruelling. After his mother returned to New
York City, Shaw roomed with a young pianist, Claude Thornhill,
with whom he formed a strong friendship, and brought him into
the Wylie band.[11]

It was while he was living in Cleveland that Shaw discovered
a stack of Louis Armstrong records at a record jobber's ware-

house. He took them home and "it was like instant *satori*. I couldn't believe what I heard. It was 'dirty' music, meaning he'd slur notes, do things that a trained musician was taught not to do. And yet it all worked." Shaw took a week off from his band job and drove to Chicago, where Armstrong was appearing at the Savoy. "The first thing I heard him play was that cadenza at the beginning of *West End Blues*. I could play it for you right now, note for note on the piano. It's in my head, indelible."[12]

In 1929, Shaw entered a local newspaper competition designed to publicize the National Air Races, with an essay on "How the National Air Races Will Benefit Cleveland," together with a thematic song for the occasion. He won the first prize—an expenses-paid trip to Hollywood. During his visit, Shaw had a brief reunion with his father—a difficult experience for both—and met some musician friends including Tony Pastor, a member of Irving Aaronson's Commanders. After six months back in Cleveland, Shaw went back to Hollywood to join Aaronson, but disliked the band's "comic" routines and costumes.

It was when Aaronson, on tour, stopped for six weeks in Chicago, that Shaw encountered such stellar jazz musicians as Jimmy Noone, Bix Beiderbecke, Bud Freeman, Gene Krupa, Muggsy Spanier, Bunny Berigan, and the young Benny Goodman—then playing with the Ben Pollack band. Shaw recalled Goodman as "a young kid just beginning to make a name for himself in the jazz world. [He] played clarinet and was said to have learned a lot from another young clarinet player around Chicago named Frank Teschemacher."[13] After finishing work with Aaronson's Commanders, Shaw would head for the South Side to sit in with the Earl Hines band, playing at the Grand Terrace. He was quickly impressed by Teschemacher's facility on three reed instruments—clarinet, tenor, and alto.

> There was an assurance about everything that he did that made you see that he himself knew where he was going all the time; and by the time he got there you began to see it for yourself, for in its own grotesque way it made a kind of musical sense, but something extremely personal and intimate to himself, something so subtle that it could never possibly have had great communicative meaning to anyone but another musician and then only to a jazz musician.[14]

Listening to such luminaries, Shaw began to appreciate one of the distinctive regional forms of musical expression— "Chicago Jazz"—that was to be disseminated by records and broadcasts across the United States.[15] It was also in Chicago that Shaw first heard serious "classical" music—coming out of a listening booth in a music store. Intrigued, he consulted the proprietor, and eventually bought records of Stravinsky's *Le Sacre du Printemps*, the *Firebird Suite*, and Debussy's *Prélude à l'après-midi d'un faune*.

> I took [them] home and began to realize that you can learn music from those guys. I didn't know who "those guys" were. I didn't make any distinction between what they did and what I was doing except that it was lots better, more complicated, much more evolved. When I began to hear Ravel's *Alborado del Gracioso* and *Daphnis and Chloe*, Stravinsky's *Petroushka* and *Le Sacre du Printemps* and Debussy's *La Mer*—these were influences.[16]

When the Aaronson band moved to New York City, Shaw's musical education took another step forward.[17] On frequent visits to Harlem, he heard and met the "stride" pianist Willie "The Lion" Smith, who was playing at Pod's and Jerry's club.

> I had never heard any piano playing like that before in my life. He used to sit there at that battered old upright and make some of the damndest music I've ever heard coming out of any instrument. And all the time his dark fingers ran nimbly over the chipped yellow keyboard, he would keep up a running accompaniment of short growls, intermittent but rhythmic— almost like little barks—as if to himself, but actually creating a sort of syncopated, drumlike, contrapuntal undercurrent to what he was doing with his fingers and hands.[18]

Shaw occasionally sat in with "The Lion" who remembered him as "a handsome young man" recently arrived in New York City, who "was having a dickens of a time getting organized in music." When the great New Orleans clarinetist and soprano saxophonist Sidney Bechet, "who was particular about clarinet players," asked whether Shaw was "a good blues man," "The Lion" answered in the affirmative.[19] During his visits to Harlem, Shaw made many friends among African-American musicians— including the young Billie Holiday and drummer Chick Webb— and relates (rather ingenuously):

> For the most part I was actually living the life of a Negro musician, adopting Negro values and attitudes, and accepting the Negro out-group point of view not only about music but life in general. In fact, on the few occasions when I was forced to realize that I was a white man, I used to wish I could actually

be a Negro. For with these people I felt a warmth and enthusiasm and friendliness, and a sense of life that had been completely lacking in most of the relationships I had ever had with members of my own race.[20]

As Burton Peretti notes, although Shaw was "not a person to believe for long that he had 'become' black"—unlike clarinetist Mezz Mezzrow—these Harlem experiences "crystallized Shaw's sense of racial equality and justice, which came into play during his years as a bandleader."[21]

Shaw also renewed contacts with those jazz musicians who had come to New York and used to gather at a club run by Jimmy Plunkett on 53rd Street. They included trombonist Jack Teagarden, guitarist Eddie Condon, drummers Gene Krupa and Dave Tough, trumpeters Wingy Manone and Max Kaminsky, pianists Joe Bushkin and Jess Stacy, and Benny Goodman who had made the move from Chicago. Kaminsky first met Shaw when they played in a "society band" for a coming out party at the Biltmore Hotel, and quickly discovered that he "was always interested in learning and improving himself. [H]is apartment was loaded with books and records."[22]

During the early 1930s, Shaw worked in several prominent dance bands, including those of Paul Specht and Red Nichols. At this period, he played alto saxophone more often than the clarinet, and was in demand as a studio musician for radio programs. Trumpeter Manny Klein heard Shaw play alto at the Famous Door on 52nd Street, and remembered him as "one of the great clarinet players [but] he was a fantastic lead alto. Benny Goodman was not."[23] As first saxophone with the Columbia

Broadcasting System (CBS) staff orchestra, Shaw earned $500 a week, and although he welcomed the chance to use his growing musical talents, he disliked the demands of sponsors and the constraints of commercials. Having achieved a measure of success, Shaw—as he would on other occasions—left the music business. As he comments in Brigitte Berman's documentary, *Time Is All You've Got*, "I became very disillusioned with music. Gradually I began to realize that my life was going nowhere." After enrolling for a brief period for extension courses at Columbia University, in 1935 he bought a farm in Erwinna, in Bucks County, Pennsylvania, acquired a business partner, and ran a firewood delivery service to Greenwich Village. He also attempted to write a novel based on the life of Bix Beiderbecke, but discovered that "the ability to write grammatically, to make sentences that sound good, or even the ability to use words skilfully, do not make a fellow a writer. I couldn't get anything on paper that lived."[24] But at later stages in his career, Shaw would return—and with more success—to the craft of writing (see chapter 5). Moving back to New York City, Shaw—who had not played a clarinet or a saxophone for twelve months—joined Roger Wolfe Kahn's orchestra, and toured as far south as New Orleans.

As already mentioned, on April 7, 1936, Joc Helbock, owner of the Onyx Club on West 52nd Street, staged a swing concert—as a benefit for the local chapter of the American Federation of Musicians—at New York's Imperial Theater. He invited Shaw, on the day after his twenty-sixth birthday, to appear with a small group during one of the intermission sets between big-band performances by the Tommy Dorsey, Casa Loma, and Bob

Crosby orchestras.[25] Shaw—who had begun to play the clarinet and string quartet compositions of Brahms and Mozart with friends—recalled:

> I was a studio musician at the time. Nobody knew me. Joe asked me to perform with a small group while they were changing the band set up. I thought, just for kicks, that I'd write a piece for clarinet and string quartet, plus a small rhythm section. Nobody had ever done that sort of jazz chamber-music thing. So I asked some of the guys at CBS and NBC if they'd run it down with me during rehearsal breaks. They agreed. So, when they liked it I asked if they'd play with me at the Imperial Theater.[26]

Performed by "Arthur Shaw's String Ensemble," the title of the piece was *Interlude in B Flat* and it received such an enthusiastic audience response that, in one re-telling, Shaw was obliged to play it again as an encore. Yet a *Down Beat* report on the proceedings asserted that "the second selection was *Japanese Sandman* and proved that [the] idea could be adapted to [a] popular selection with plenty of guts." Apparently unaware that Glenn Miller had experimented with a string section one year before the Imperial Theater performance, Shaw later commented that "what seemed to have caught the attention of those who heard it was the enormous contrast between the combination of instruments I had used, as against what was being used around that time in jazz music." If Shaw's instrumentation was not an innovation, it still produced a sensation. British-born jazz critic Leonard Feather wrote that "Artie's one number, *Interlude in B Flat* broke up the show." Scenting (and promoting) a new superstar in the making, *Down Beat* dutifully reported that Shaw's performance at the Imperial Theater "will probably keep [Benny] Goodman awake for several nights to come. Absolutely masterful (*sic*) on technique and tone [Shaw] rates with Goodman any day. Applause tore down the house and necessitated many a bow."[27]

Whatever its provenance, Shaw's string combo marked a turning point in his career. After the concert, Tommy Rockwell—of the Rockwell-O'Keefe booking agency—pressed him to form a permanent group. Shaw's first band, billed as "Art Shaw and his Orchestra," consisted of two trumpets, a trombone, tenor saxophone, clarinet, and a conventional rhythm section, plus the Imperial Theater format of two violins, a viola, and a cello. It opened at the Silver Grill in the Lexington Hotel in New York City in the summer of 1936 and was flagged as "A Dance Orchestra Combining At the Same Time a Complete Swing Band With a Dreamy String Ensemble." *Metronome* critic George T. Simon gave the band a favorable "A-minus" notice:

> What Shaw has done is to build a star band that can do a neat job on both swing and schmaltz, and at times even combine some of the elements of each. Shaw can deliver quite an adequate brand of Dixieland, while just the presence of the strings helps to appease and even satisfy those folks who have drifted into the room but who don't want to care much for this newfangled thing called swing.

Simon commended Shaw's arrangers, Joe Lipman and Jerry Gray, and suggested that the leader's clarinet style, while similar to Benny Goodman's, also displayed distinct originality. Less accurately, Simon predicted a successful future for Shaw's new venture "not only because he has accomplished so much in such a short space of time, but also because what he has accomplished is in the exceptional class."[28]

In fact, the public was less than enthused about Shaw's "strings and swing" combination. Reflecting on this period with some justifiable bitterness, Shaw remembered that neither agents nor audiences warmed to his novel instrumentation. "Nobody would accept the idea of a jazz band built around a string quartet. I had to do most of the arranging myself. Nobody was writing for string quartets and small jazz bands."[29]

Critics are divided on the merits or otherwise of Shaw's studio recordings for the Brunswick label with his 1936–1937 band. Some argue that they project a stiff rhythm, and are ill served by the interludes, transitions, introductions, and codas played by the string quartet. Others consider the performances of such titles as *Thou Swell*, *Copenhagen*, *Streamline*, *Sweet Lorraine*, and *Sobbin' Blues* to have a freshness and vitality, with the strings adding a certain astringency to the overall sound. Shaw himself, who never entirely gave up his fascination with the use of strings in a jazz/swing context, has always regarded his first band with parental affection.

> This first band of mine was virtually two different types of musical combinations playing together as one. The problem was to write for the strings in such a way as to realize their particular kind of tone colour, without interfering with the strictly jazz part of the band and yet adding something, so as to make an advantage of the strong section without having to limit the jazz quality of the over-all musical effect.[30]

When the band played at the Adolphus Hotel in Dallas, business was so poor that the management cancelled its engagement. On March 4, 1937, this first Shaw orchestra made its final recordings—sixteen titles for the RCA Thesaurus series, broadcast over the NBC radio network.

After another disappointing engagement in New Jersey, early in 1937, Shaw—doubtless aware of Benny Goodman's recent (and stringless) success—formed a second orchestra, and vowed that it would be "the loudest band in the whole goddam world." This was a fourteen-piece aggregation, now advertised as "Art Shaw and His New Music." In at least one respect, it marked an improvement over the first edition: the fine rhythm section featured Al Avola (guitar), Ben Ginsberg (bass), Cliff Leeman (drums), and Les Burness (piano). The band opened at the Roseland Ballroom in Boston in April 1936, where it received "airshot" broadcasts twice a week and included trumpeter John Best, trombonists George Arus and Harry Rogers, and saxophonists Les Robinson and Tony Pastor. As the new band began to take shape, Shaw developed and refined a basic concept for its repertoire: the compositions of composers such as Jerome Kern, Cole Porter, Richard Rogers, Vincent Youmans, Sigmund Romberg, George Gershwin, and Irving Berlin. He later explained: "What I intended to do was to take the best of this popular Americana and arrange it in the best way I could. I wasn't aiming at any so-called style. Each tune would more or less dictate the style of its own arrangement."[31]

In addition to airshots, the second Shaw band made eight commercial recording sessions for the Brunswick Company, playing arrangements (mostly by Shaw himself) of such popular tunes of the time as *Night and Day* and *I Surrender Dear*, while a session of September 17, 1937, featured the scat vocalist Leo Watson on *Shoot the Likker to Me, John Boy*. Shaw's theme tune, the moody and aptly titled *Nightmare*, was also made on this date. The following month, the band recorded two Shaw originals, *Non-Stop Flight* and *Free For All*, which—together with *The Blues March* (originally issued as both sides of a 78-rpm record—revealed Shaw's maturing instrumental style, marked by his increasing exploration of the upper octave of the clarinet register.[32] The band also went on tour and Shaw ruefully recalled:

> We hit the road in an old truck we had bought from Tommy Dorsey. It had Tommy's name painted on both sides, weather-beaten but legible. Until we had enough money to pay for re-painting the body, we were stopped three times for having stolen it. A cop in Boston arrested our Negro driver and tossed him into the can. He had heard Tommy Dorsey broadcasting from New York an hour before. We left our driver in jail, the truck in the police yard, and went on to our next stand by bus.[33]

In what was to be a momentous decision, Shaw hired Billie Holiday as the band's vocalist in 1938. Max Kaminsky, who played with Shaw from January to June of that year, claims that when Shaw was late for the band's first rehearsal in Boston: "I started the band on a new arrangement [of] *Yesterdays* [and] asked Billie to sing the clarinet solo part to fill in for Artie. On the second time around, she came gliding in, in the nick of time. While she was singing, Artie walked in, and he just stood there. He couldn't believe she was that good."[34] Kaminsky's anecdote, while dramatically apposite, also suggests a highly selective memory. Shaw had been present as a sideman on four Billie Holiday studio sessions in July 1936, and had been so impressed that he had suggested that she join the band which he was forming. Aware of the problems that she would face in an all-white orchestra, Billie had declined the invitation. Again, Shaw, as mentioned, had been a regular visitor to Pod's and Jerry's club in Harlem. In the "Arena" TV production "The Long Night of Lady Day" he states that on one occasion he heard a young African-American girl sing the blues "and she really had a sense of time and a sense of phrasing that was jazz in the best sense of the word." Willie "The Lion" Smith had informed him, "That's Billie Holiday. She drinks too much and gets fired from too many jobs, but she can sing." When Holiday left the Count Basie orchestra, Shaw immediately offered her a job because "she was a good singer. I wouldn't have hired her if she wasn't. She was looking for work and I could afford her—she wasn't that well-known back then." In his autobiography, Shaw says that at this period Billie "a young, healthy kid only about seventeen or so at the time I first met her [was] already beginning to develop that distinctive style of hers which has been copied and imitated by so many singers of popular music that the average listener of today cannot realise how original she actually is."[35]

Problems and racial tensions plagued Billie's nine-month tenure with Shaw. Her first appearance with the band was at Boston's Roseland-State Ballroom, on March 15, 1938, for a three-month engagement. One press report noted that "the contract given to Billie to act as part of this outfit is an indefinite one, and unless racial prejudices intervene, she will remain with the band from now on."[36] But the Schribman Brothers booking agency—which had underwritten Shaw's engagement—was not comfortable backing a white orchestra with a black singer. In her autobiography, Billie relates:

> The sight of sixteen men on a bandstand with a Negro girl singer had never been seen before—in Boston or anywhere. The question of how the public would take to it had to be faced on opening night at Roseland. Naturally, Sy Schribman was worried. But Artie was a guy who never thought in terms of white and coloured. "I can take care of the situation," was his answer. "And I know Lady can take care of herself."[37]

The Holiday/Shaw partnership was a musically happy one. Two months after she joined the band, *Metronome* reported that "the addition of Billie Holiday to Shaw's band has put this outfit in top brackets. Her lilting vocals jibe beautifully with the Shaw style; and her stuff is going big with the customers. The personality and musicianship of this real jazz gal have won and unified the whole band, and more than one solo is being played straight at Billie." But in a sharply dissenting opinion, "White Man's Jazz No Good for Holiday?" *Down Beat* commented:

> Billie Holiday is still singing with Artie Shaw, but it is a damn shame she has to waste her talents with a band of that caliber. Understand, in spite of Cliff Leeman's pseudo-sizzle cymbal, Artie has a swell outfit, but they don't show off Billie any. Naturally they play white man's jazz and that's no backing for Billie's singing, which, even during its more commercial moments, has a definite "race" flavour. When she had Count Basie behind her, the girl was right. Now she's as incongruous

as a diamond set in a rosette of old cantaloupe rinds with coffee grounds.[38]

Writing in *Down Beat*, John Hammond commented that although Benny Goodman's recently revised band "has something no other white band can touch, the combination of Artie and Billie makes me feel that Benny is going to have to watch out for himself."[39] But there were also problems. Song-pluggers pressured Shaw not to allow Billie to sing their songs over the radio, because of her deviations from the written melodies. And she was not allowed to sit on the stand with the band's white singer, Helen Forrest.

When the Shaw band toured the southern states, Holiday encountered the degrading practices and customs of racial segregation and discrimination. She became sick of repeated scenes in roadside diners where she was often not even allowed to eat in the kitchen. "Sometimes it was a choice between me eating and the whole band starving. I got tired of having a federal case over breakfast, lunch and dinner."[40] Shaw was well aware of Billie's volatile nature when confronted by racial bigotry, and in *The Long Night of Lady Day* remembers warning her to expect trouble in the South, and promising to help if things got out of hand. At one southern location, Billie sang *Travelin'* with the band—to the delight of the white audience who wanted an encore. One patron kept yelling "Have the nigger wench sing another song," which Shaw (correctly) interpreted as a redneck expression of critical approval. Billie, understandably outraged, leaned forward and mouthed the expletive "motherfucker" to the offending patron. "It looked like pandemonium. This guy saw her—he couldn't believe what he saw. He heard the word. She used to get very salty with people like that."

Shaw has also related that "as a gag we once got Billie into a hotel by painting a little red dot on her forehead between her eyes. Two guys carried her bags. She got the room not as a black person or a coloured person, but as an Indian." Billie remembered how Shaw propelled her into the largest hotel in a small Kentucky town by having eight band members escort her to the desk, "like it was as natural as breathing. I think the man at the desk figured it couldn't be true what he thought he saw, and I couldn't be a Negro or nobody would act like that. I think they thought I was Spanish or something, so they gave me a nice room and no back talk."[41]

Not all the Shaw/Holiday appearances were marred by racial tensions. On October 17, 1938, they performed a benefit concert at the Savoy Ballroom in Chicago, sponsored by the African-American newspaper, the Chicago *Defender* for the Negro Christmas Basket Fund. Posters for the event proclaimed that Billie Holiday "America's First Lady of Song" would be appearing with Artie Shaw "King of Clarinet Players." As *Billboard* duly reported:

> Local Harlemites (*sic*) coughed up close to $3,500 last Monday eve to swing and sway to Artie Shaw. All attendance records were broken and Artie with his sepia songstress Billie Holiday had to work an extra half hour after pleading with the throng to go home. The crowd couldn't get enough of Shaw's jiving—a surprise to Rockwell O'Keefe as Shaw is still not a name in this sector.[42]

But Billie ran into racial discrimination later in the same month when she appeared with Shaw at the Blue Room of the Lincoln Hotel in New York City. Maria Kramer, the hotel's manager and owner, would not allow her to enter the Blue Room through the main entrance, but made her come up through the kitchen. Billie told a reporter from the *Amsterdam News*, "I was billed next to Artie himself, but was never allowed to visit the bar or the dining room as did other members of the band [and] had to remain alone in a little dark room all evening until I was called on to do my numbers. And these numbers became fewer and fewer as the night went on."[43] Shaw's recollection is that Maria Kramer complained to him that Billie was using the public elevator to get to her dressing room and that southern guests had objected that the Lincoln was "taking coloured." Shortly after the episode, Billie left Shaw, blaming his managers for her problems.

The circumstances of her departure aroused considerable comment. The columnist Walter Winchell wrote that Billie's friend and mentor, John Hammond, "was sitting in the Lincoln Hotel supper room enjoying Artie Shaw's band not knowing Billie had given her notice two days before. The outside billboards, however, still stated that she was among the Lincoln's attractions." In a 1993 interview, Shaw told Stuart Nicholson that "the press were on to me at that time; they said I fired her because she was black, conveniently overlooking that when I hired her she was black too! I've been castigated for hiring her; I was told I was exploiting a black person. I was not exploiting her, I was doing the best I could to present her in an impartial light as a musician singing with my band."[44]

Despite an acrimonious departure from Shaw—in one interview she claimed the Lincoln incident was the occasion but not the cause of her departure and that "I simply got enough of Artie's snooty, know-it-all mannerisms"—Holiday retained affectionate memories of their close friendship.

> There aren't many people who fought harder than Artie against the vicious people in the music business or the crummy side of second-class citizenship which eats at the guts of so many musicians. He didn't win. But he didn't lose either. It wasn't long after I left him that he told them to shove it like I had. And people still talk about him as if he were nuts because there were things more important to him than a million damn bucks a year.[45]

Shaw, for his part, stated later that:

> My band was obviously a rather strange place for her to be, our music wasn't like any of the music she sang with. It worked, but in a very strange way, and oddly enough a lot of people didn't like it. RCA for example. When she left my band, it was a mutual agreement. She was under contract to me and I offered to finance her act and buy her gowns and arrangements. We remained good friends to the day of her death.[46]

With exposure on records, broadcasts from the Roseland Ballroom and its nationwide tours, Shaw's orchestra had begun to attract critical attention in the musical press. Not all of the notices were favorable. One Boston writer criticized the band for playing a thirty-five minute version of the blues, and accused

Shaw of having claimed that he would be the new "King of Swing" within a year. Shaw rebutted the charge in an indignant and revealing letter to *Metronome*:

> My personal craving for success and the contributions I wish to make to swing music do not hinge upon my being crowned "King." There is room for twenty, even fifty swing bands, and I say more power to any contemporary leader who makes an outstanding success. If I were writing a novel, I wouldn't particularly want to be known as the greatest novelist. I'd have satisfaction if my book were judged a success on its own and not on a basis of comparison and that's how I feel about my music. I want the public to recognize me, naturally, but I gain plenty of personal satisfaction without necessarily bowling over all rival orchestras. I'd like to deny that ["King of Swing"] statement because I personally would have contempt for any individual who made such a pompous, bombastic announcement.[47]

In the course of a long and excruciatingly written review of the band in the November 1938 issue of *Swing* magazine, its reporter observed:

> There's a new Pied Piper coming over the swing horizon. He's dark-haired, young and collegiate and he plays a brand of dansapation that grows on jitterbugs and schmaltz-lovers alike. He's Artie Shaw. It didn't seem possible that with Pied Piper Benny Goodman still having swing's children dog his heels in throngs, another fellow playing a black bubble-pipe could take a top-ranking place in the musical sun, but that man Shaw is doing it fast.[48]

In the same year, Shaw was invited to record for the RCA Victor Company, who renamed him *Artie* Shaw—allegedly because a Victor executive said that *Art* Shaw sounded like a sneeze. Among the first titles recorded by "Artie Shaw and His Orchestra" on July 24, 1938, were *Indian Love Call* (featuring a hoarse vocal by Tony Pastor), *Back Bay Shuffle*, and Billie Holiday's only known studio session with the Shaw band, *Any Old Time*, which was not released for some years because of contractual problems. In conversation with broadcaster Fred Hall, Shaw recalled the events surrounding *Any Old Time*—which he had written and arranged.

> That came about when we were off a couple of nights on the road doing one-night stands—and we were in a town, near Binghamton, New York, and there's not a hell of a lot you can do of an evening in Binghamton. Billie Holiday was with the band, and I thought I'd write a tune for her. When we went to record it. RCA wouldn't release it, so I went to Billie and said, "Look, they don't want to release the record, so I guess that if I want the tune released at all, I'll have to do it with someone else." So I did it with Helen Forrest, and they released that.[49]

Barry Kernfeld suggests plausibly that in her rendition of *Any Old Time*, Holiday "perhaps out of courtesy to the composer and leader, stays closer to the shape of Shaw's melody than she might have done with her own and [pianist] Teddy Wilson's groups, but she gives its rhythm her usual treatment, floating across and around the beat." Kernfeld also notes that in Shaw's arrangement, the instrumental passage immediately before Holiday's vocal anticipates the theme of Glenn Miller's *String of Pearls*,

composed and arranged by Jerry Gray three years after the Shaw/
Holiday performance.[50]

But it was Shaw's recording (at the same session as *Any Old
Time*) of the longest popular song ever written—a tune with a
remarkable 108-bar structure—which was to catapult him to national (and international) prominence. And, as Shaw confirms, it
happened almost by accident.

> Everybody around the RCA Victor studio thought we had a hit
> record. As it turned out, the RCA people were quite wrong.
> *Indian Love Call* had an enormous sale, but that wasn't be-
> cause it was a hit. It just happened to be on the other side of
> a nice little tune of Cole Porter's.

The "nice little tune" was *Begin the Beguine*, the recording
of which Shaw has identified as "my real turning point"; yet the
circumstances were hardly auspicious and in the end pure seren-
dipity ruled. Shaw remembers that the song had died "a fast
death" after a brief appearance on Broadway in a flop musical
show called *Jubilee*.

> I had just happened to like it so I insisted on recording it at
> this first session, in spite of the recording manager who
> thought it a complete waste of time and only let me make it
> after I argued that it would at least make a nice quiet contrast
> to *Indian Love Call*.[51]

The eventual—and massive—success of *Begin the Beguine*
(it sold over a million copies) provided Shaw with "a new
status"—one, which he claims, obliged him "to learn to function

in a new way." In his witty and opinionated study, *American Popular Song*, Alec Wilder writes of Cole Porter's composition:

> [It] is a maverick, an unprecedented experiment, and one which, to this day, after hearing it hundreds of times, I cannot sing or whistle or play from start to finish without the printed music. I suppose it conjures up for the listener all sorts of romantic memories embodying the ultimate tropical evening and the most dramatic dance floors ever imagined [But] along about the sixtieth measure I find myself muttering another title, *End the Beguine*.[52]

Yet that "new way" was already in evidence in the recording itself, which is notably audacious and imaginative. Shaw changed the original beguine tempo into a modified 4/4 and then "began the beguine" with a unison brass statement coordinated with a single snare-drum shot on the downbeat of the first bar. An infectious riff provides the setting for Shaw's dazzling solo entrance. The remainder of this seminal recording consists of statements and restatements of the theme by Shaw, the full ensemble, the saxophone and trombone sections, and Tony Pastor's tenor. The whole performance is anchored by drummer Cliff Leeman's 4/4 swing combined with rimshots and splash cymbals—most clearly evident behind Pastor's solo. Most importantly, *Begin the Beguine* made Artie Shaw, at the age of twenty-eight, into a dazzling new star in the Swing firmament, and catapulted him "into the very situation he'd dreaded most."[53]

NOTES

1. Maldwyn A. Jones, *Destination America* (London: Weidenfeld and Nicholson, 1976), 173, 176.

2. Benny Goodman and Irving Kolodin, *The Kingdom of Swing* (New York: Frederick Ungar Publishing Company, 1961), 15; 17–19. For accounts of Goodman's early years, see James Lincoln Collier, *Benny Goodman and the Swing Era* (New York: Oxford University Press, 1989), 1–12, and Ross Firestone, *Swing, Swing, Swing: The Life and Times of Benny Goodman* (London: Hodder and Stoughton, 1993), 17–35.

3. Firestone, 19.

4. Artie Shaw, *The Trouble With Cinderella: An Outline of Identity* (New York: Da Capo Press, 1979), 22–3.

5. Burton W. Peretti, *The Creation of Jazz: Music, Race, and Culture in Urban America* (Urbana and Chicago: University of Chicago Press, 1992), 90.

6. *Ibid.* 74.

7. Edmund L. Blandford, *Artie Shaw: A Bio-Discography* (Hastings, Sussex: Castle Books, 1973), 11.

8. George T. Simon, *The Big Bands*, 391.

9. *The Semantics of Jazz: A Symposium*. Moderator, Artie Shaw. California Lutheran University, Sept. 12, 1987. Transcript in author's possession.

10. Robert Lewis Taylor, "Middle-Aged Man Without a Horn," *The New Yorker*, May 19, 1962, 50.

11. Thornhill was to lead a subtle and intelligent band during and after World War II, and inspired Miles Davis, Gerry Mulligan, and pianist-arranger Gil Evans in the "Birth of the Cool Band" of the 1950s.

12. Ted Berkman, "Why Artie Walked," *Santa Barbara: The Magazine of Santa Barbara County* (February/March 1986), 56.

13. *The Trouble With Cinderella*, 197.

14. *Ibid.* 199

15. For the evolution of jazz in Chicago and the relations between black and white musicians, see William Howland Kenney's excellent study: *Chicago Jazz: A Cultural History, 1904–1930* (New York and Oxford: Oxford University Press, 1993).

16. Henry Duckham, "A Masterclass With Artie Shaw," *The Clarinet* 12 (1985), 11.

17. Shaw's arrival in New York City was not without incident. He was involved in an accident when a pedestrian walked in front of his

car and was fatally injured. Lengthy police enquiries were to exonerate him from blame, but when Aaronson left without him, Shaw, now nineteen and unemployed, had to wait six months before he was eligible for membership of the local chapter of the American Federation of Musicians.

18. *The Trouble With Cinderella*, 224. Shaw's description of "The Lion" is close to Duke Ellington's memoir of his first encounter with the pianist at the Capitol Palace in New York City. "My first impression of The Lion—even before I saw him—was the thing I felt as I walked down the steps. A strange thing. A square-type fellow might say, 'This joint is jumping,' but to those who had become acclimatized—the tempo was the lope—actually everything and everybody seemed to be doing whatever they were doing in the tempo The Lion's group was laying down. The waiters served in that tempo; everybody who had to walk in, out, or around the place walked with a beat." *Music Is My Mistress* (New York: Doubleday, 1973), 90.

19. Willie "The Lion" Smith and George Hoefer, *Music on My Mind: The Memoirs of an American Pianist* (London: The Jazz Book Club, 1966), 169. "The Lion" adds that "Artie used to encourage me to get my tunes written down and published. Later when Artie had his first band, he recorded some of my numbers. He featured the introduction to my tune *Music on My Mind* under a new title, *I've Got the Misery.*" 170.

20. *The Trouble With Cinderella*, 228–9.

21. Peretti, *The Creation of Jazz*, 207.

22. Max Kaminsky with V. E. Hughes, *My Life in Jazz* (New York: Harper and Row, 1963), 94.

23. Arnold Shaw, *52nd Street: The Street of Jazz* (New York: Da Capo Press, 1977), 116.

24. *The Trouble With Cinderella*, 262.

25. The other major attractions at this concert included Louis Armstrong and his Orchestra, Red Nichols and his Five Pennies, Bunny Berigan and his Swing Gang, and violinist Stuff Smith and his Onyx Club Band.

26. Liner notes by Artie Shaw to the Book-of-the-Month Club record set *Artie Shaw: The Legacy* (Camp Hill, Pennsylvania: 1984). This

compilation purports to include a digitally re-mastered recording of his performance at the Imperial Theater. (See Chapter 7). According to the printed program, Shaw's ensemble included Harry Bluestone and Emanuel "Mannie" Green (violins), "Izzie" Zir (viola), "Rudy" Sims (cello), Carl Kress (guitar), and Arthur Stein (drums).

27. *The Trouble With Cinderella*, 299. Firestone, *Swing, Swing, Swing*, 177. Richard M. Sudhalter, *Lost Chords*, 577.

28. George T. Simon, *Simon Says*, 68–70. Simon also commended the Shaw's band's "showmanship angle." Shaw himself, "a clean-cut looking chap, presents a pleasing, reserved front. Quite obviously, he knows what the dancers want for not only does he contrast his tempos nicely, but he also sets tempos that are thoroughly danceable." Reflecting on this 1936 review years later, Simon added: "To anyone who has watched Artie on those TV talk shows, 'reserved' is sure a misnomer."

29. Chip Deffaa, *Swing Legacy* (Metuchen, New Jersey: The Scarecrow Press and the Institute of Jazz Studies, Rutgers University, 1989), 23.

30. *The Trouble With Cinderella*, 302. He adds: "There was no room for the sort of musical subtleties I was trying to create with this atypical little band. Those were the days of the tousled-haired, eye-rolling, gum-chewing drummers—those boys who hit everything in sight except the customers. A new fad had swept the nation. If a band couldn't play good music, it could always call itself a 'swing band' and play *loud* music instead." *Ibid*. 310.

31. *Ibid*. 331.

32. Max Kaminsky claims that initially Shaw's band was "very immature and had no definite style. The players became very great later on— Tony Pastor, Chuck Peterson, Cliff Leeman—but at that time they were unseasoned and inexperienced. Their worst trouble was learning to play in time, and except for Tony Pastor, they didn't know much about jazz or swing." *My Life in Jazz*, 96.

33. Chris Albertson, "Artie Shaw," Liner notes for *The Swing Era, 1937–1938* (New York: Time-Life Records), 38; The *Trouble With Cinderella*, 328.

34. *My Life in Jazz*, 97.

35. Stuart Nicholson, *Billie Holiday* (London: Victor Gollancz, 1995), 99. See also: Donald Clarke, *Wishing on the Moon: The Life and Times of Billie Holiday* (London: Penguin Books, 1995), 140, and John White, *Billie Holiday: Her Life and Times* (Tunbridge Wells: Spellmount Books, 1987), 68–9. *The Trouble With Cinderella*, 230.

36. Ken Vail, *Lady Day's Diary: The Life of Billie Holiday 1937–1959* (Castle Communications: Chessington, Surrey, 1996), 19.

37. Billie Holiday with William Dufty, *Lady Sings the Blues* (London: Sphere Books Edition, 1973), 69. In fact, June Richmond, described by George T. Simon as "an extremely effervescent and very large coloured gal" had appeared in public with the Jimmy Dorsey band, early in 1938. *The Big Bands*, 150.

38. *Metronome*, May 1938. *Down Beat*, August 1935, 5.

39. Firestone, *Swing, Swing, Swing*, 231.

40. *Lady Sings the Blues*, 73.

41. *Ibid.* 70.

42. *Lady Day's Diary*, 26.

43. John Chilton, *Billie's Blues* (London: Quartet Books, 1975), 57.

44. Nicholson, *Billie Holiday*, 106.

45. *Lady Sings the Blues*, 80. Billie would often drive to engagements with Shaw in his newly acquired Rolls Royce, and they became very close—although there is no evidence that they were ever lovers. "Sometimes I'd walk into his hotel suite and take one look at him and know that that day he was Mister Shaw and he didn't want to be messed with. Other days he was "Old Man" or "Artie." Sometimes he would want to get lost on his farm without shaving for months, staying in this one pair of overalls, the way he did when he wrote *Back Bay Shuffle*." *Ibid.* 78. Billie also referred to Shaw—who suffered from bad breath, as "Breath." Drummer Cliff Leeman relates that after Shaw had gone to the Catskills and attempted to write, he hadn't shaved for two months, and liked to say "before I came back to New York I looked like Jesus Christ." Billie was sarcastically unimpressed by this repeated anecdote, and "whenever she had the chance she used to say 'Jesus Christ, His Clarinet and His Orchestra.'" Clarke, *Wishing on the Moon*, 142.

46. Chilton, *Billie's Blues*, 59–60. Critic Leonard Feather, writing in the *Melody Maker*, suggested that "Holiday left Shaw because (a) His new radio sponsors, the "Old Gold" cigarette people, refused to use her on the air—maybe because Billie smokes a different kind of cigarette and (b) she was made to enter the Lincoln Hotel, where the band plays, by the back door." *Ibid*. 58.

47. Simon, *The Big Bands*, 416.

48. Blandford, *Artie Shaw*, 50–51.

49. Fred Hall, *Dialogues In Swing: Intimate Conversations With Stars of the Big Band Era* (Ventura, California: Pathfinder Publishing, 1989), 133. The lyrics of *Any Old Time* also contained allusions to other popular songs—*Stormy Weather*, *Through the Years*, and *Yours and Mine*—the last title had been recorded by Holiday with Teddy Wilson in 1937. Shaw recalled that "I did that as a sort of stunt. Billie was joining the band, and I wanted to give her a song she could sing. You'd be surprised—or maybe not—how few people caught it." Sudhalter, *Lost Chords* 823, Note 39.

50. Barry Kernfeld, "Big Bands," in Kernfeld, ed., *The Blackwell Guide to Recorded Jazz* (Oxford: Blackwell Publishers, 1992), 127. In conversation with Chip Deffaa, Shaw remarked: "My band didn't have a quote, *style*. I didn't have, for example, that thing that Glenn Miller had—that one thing, that monotonous sound. We used it sometimes— the end of *Any Old Time*, which I wrote and arranged for Billie had the clarinet over the saxophones. But that wasn't a thing we foisted on every tune." *Swing Legacy*, 27. Shaw retains a healthy contempt for Glenn Miller's saccharine and decidedly un-swinging sound, and told Fred Hall, "I don't like to be [a] revisionist on history, but I think that band was like the beginning of the end. It was a mechanized version of what they call jazz music. I still can't stand to listen to it. But that's the one of the period that everybody buys, for some reason." *Dialogues in Swing*. 144.

51. *The Trouble With Cinderella*, 33–4.

52. *Ibid*. 335. *American Popular Music: The Great Innovators 1900– 1950* (New York: Oxford University Press, 1972), 240.

53. Sudhalter, 820, Note 15.

Still from *The Dancing Co-ed*, 1939

Beginning the Beguine:
$ucce$$ and Remorse

When I was a kid I played clarinet, and my first influence was Artie Shaw. I heard him play on records and the radio, and I thought he played beautifully, with a wonderful sound and a great technique. Then I saw a picture of him. He was going to be married to a movie star. She was beautiful. He seemed very glamorous to me. And I never doubted for a second that I could be as great as Artie Shaw.

Art Pepper, *Straight Life: The Story of Art Pepper*

When the Shaw band stopped off to play a prom at Indiana University in the summer of 1938, there were repeated requests for *Begin the Beguine*, which had just been released (unknown to Shaw) by RCA. It was to become his greatest hit and second signature tune. Trumpeter Bernie Privin recalled: "I joined the band three weeks after *Begin the Beguine* became available in the stores. Before I knew it, the band was the hottest thing in the country. The record was played everywhere. Because of it, Artie suddenly became a major celebrity."[1] Some time after the record had climbed into the American Hit Parade, Shaw met Cole Porter, who remarked cheerfully "I'm glad to meet my collaborator."[2]

Nearly sixty years since its appearance, Shaw's interpretation of *Begin the Beguine* still retains its freshness, excitement, and sensuality, and confounds Owen Peterson's peevish comment that "listening today [1969] to *Beguine*, it's difficult to imagine what all the fuss was about. It isn't as musically outstanding as many later Shaw recordings, and it isn't in the same league as Glenn Miller's *American Patrol*."[3] Gunther Schuller—by no means an unqualified admirer of Shaw's oeuvre—writes that his solo on *Beguine* demonstrates Shaw's "ability to spin long, elegant, vibrant, seamless lines, almost as if he were trying to capture on his clarinet what a violin, without the need to breathe, could do so naturally and effectively." He also notes Shaw's unstinted admiration for the violinist Jascha Heifetz.[4]

Jerry Gray's arrangement of the Cole Porter song certainly contributed to its musical quality, with a masterly blending of textures, ensemble passages, and interspersed solos. As mentioned, in arranging Porter's tune, Gray had substituted a modified 4/4 beat for the original beguine rhythm, and dancers at Roseland State Ballroom had responded enthusiastically to the innovation. Gray himself remarked, "I felt I had to get the attention of the dancers in the ballroom, and that's why I wrote that hard introduction."[5] Gray was also a contributor to Shaw's later successes, with splendid arrangements of such titles as *Lover Come Back to Me*, *Jumpin' on the Merry-Go-Round*, *Who's Excited?*, and *Prelude in C Major*.

Schuller feels that Shaw has given insufficient credit to his arrangers. Unlike other leaders, he either did not recognize or would not admit "that the style of the band is determined unequivocally by the arranger, not the leader (unless the leader is also the style-setting arranger)." Again, Schuller maintains that Gray's scores for the 1939 Shaw band were less cluttered and more spacious that either Shaw's own or those of his earlier writers. "Gray's arrangements were full of contrasts of color, of texture, of dynamics, breaking up the old formularized arranging roles into new and different ensemble combinations. [He] took the trumpets out of the top-of-the-staff upper range, using them instead in all kinds of registers, mutings, dynamic levels, and timbral mixtures." With similar voicings for the reeds, Gray's charts "lent themselves to a more *swinging* performance style" better suited to the dancing craze that swept America during the swing era.[6]

Schuller's analysis of Gray's contribution to the success of the 1939 Shaw band is judicious, but his contention that Shaw did not appreciate it is erroneous, since he [Shaw] has stated:

> Jerry came very close to being to me what Billy Strayhorn was to Duke [Ellington]. He was a pupil and he was a friend. I taught him how to arrange. I was an arranger before I was a band leader. Jerry started with my string band in 1936. He was my first violinist. And he played some jazz accordion. Later, in 1939, when I broke up the band, I called Glenn Miller and told him that I had a few people he ought to listen to. He hired Johnny Best on trumpet and he hired Jerry [who] did Glenn a lot of good. Jerry wrote A *String of Pearls* for him.[7]

From July 1938 to November 1939, the Shaw band recorded prolifically for RCA Victor, under the terms of a contract which guaranteed him a minimum of $100,000 over two years. The remakes of *Non-Stop Flight* and *Nightmare* are superior to the earlier Brunswick versions, and with *Lover Come Back to Me,* recorded in January 1939, Shaw's band reached levels of precision, quality, and drive that equalled those of Benny Goodman's contemporary offerings.

Musicians and fans were divided in their loyalties to Goodman and Shaw. Goodman was often said to possess a better jazz sense, while Shaw was judged to have greater harmonic and high-register skills. Goodman himself reportedly said of Shaw during this period: "He knows his instrument well, has extreme development in both registers, and an amazing harmonic sense."[8] Whitney Balliett observes that during the 1930s, "Goodman and Shaw governed from opposite poles. Goodman, an arpeggio player, had great facility and passion. He had a fine tone and was a first-class melodist. [He] seemed one of the finest of all jazz players. Artie Shaw was cooler, narrower, and deeper. He was an even better melodist, and though his tone was smaller than Goodman's, he was more interesting harmonically. Musicians tended to relish Shaw."[9]

The drummer Buddy Rich provided much of the Shaw band's new drive. Formerly with Harry James, Rich ignited the ensemble with his ability and enthusiasm, often urging on his colleagues with vocal exhortations—even on studio recordings like the roaring *Traffic Jam*. Rich had been a member of trumpeter Bunny Berigan's band, and tenor saxophonist George Auld, who left Berigan to join Shaw, introduced him to the exciting young drummer. Shaw agreed to let Rich play a set with the band at the Blue Room of the Hotel Lincoln. But critic George Simon, during the course of a largely positive review of the band's performances in *Down Beat* (February 1939), was less than happy with drummer Cliff Leeman's new replacement.

Buddy Rich is a brilliant percussionist, he has tremendous technique, he's steady and he gets a fine swing, but, like so many drummers who've grown up in the [Gene] Krupa era, he's cursed with the misconception that the drummer is supposed to do more than supply a good background. As a result, Buddy in his enthusiasm plays too much drums, consequently breaking up the general rhythmic effect.[10]

In a 1992 interview, Shaw himself appears to have shared Simon's estimate of the rambunctious young Buddy Rich.

When he first came in the band he used to throw everything he had into every chorus, playing like the Czechoslovakian army. I taught him that it was better to start quiet and then build up. Eventually I talked him into quitting [in 1939] when I told him that he was playing much more for himself than for the band.

Shaw is not entirely consistent in his evaluations of Buddy Rich. For example, he told George Simon that although Rich "had enormous energy, enormous vitality in his playing," he was a totally undisciplined musician. "The hardest job was to keep him within the bounds of what I was trying to get the ensemble to do." Yet after settling in to his new surroundings, "he made the band into a practically new band overnight. I was quite grateful to him." Shaw has also been quoted as saying:

When Buddy came in the band, in 1939, he couldn't read music—and, for that matter, I don't think he could read any better at the end of his life. I told him that some of our arrangements were pretty complex. He asked me if he could sit out front a couple of nights and learn the arrangements. He

did, and said he was ready, and he was—amazingly so. He was
an amusing, ebullient kid, and sometimes he'd get so excited
when he was playing that he'd yell and rush the beat. Near the
end of the year he was with the band, he began going off on
his own in his playing, doing things that were good for him but
not for the band. I sat him down and told him what he'd begun
doing, and not long after that we parted amicably. He went
with Tommy Dorsey, which was just right, because Tommy
had a big show band.[11]

Recalling his one-year tenure with the Shaw orchestra, Rich
told his friend and biographer, Mel Tormé: "They were all in
shock when I came on the band. No drummer had ever punctuated brass licks with the bass drum before. All of a sudden, I
come along, kicking the band right up its ass with bass drum ac-
cents. They couldn't believe it, but they liked it."[12]

Whatever the peccadilloes of its dynamic drummer, the solo
strength of the band had been greatly improved with the arrival
(in December 1938) of trumpeter Bernie Privin and tenor saxophonist George Auld. Brooklyn-born Privin had played local engagements with Harry Reser's band, before joining successively
the orchestras of Bunny Berigan, Tommy Dorsey, and Jan Savitt.[13] Auld, born in Toronto, had moved to New York in 1929,
where he won a Rudy Wiedoeft Scholarship in 1931, and studied
with the alto teacher for nine months. After hearing Coleman
Hawkins's recording of *Meditation*, Auld switched to tenor saxophone and came to prominence with Bunny Berigan's orchestra
in 1937–1938. A hard-driving tenor player in the Hawkins-Ben
Webster tradition, Auld was later a member of Benny Goodman's
orchestra and sextet. Mel Tormé, who cites Shaw's band of 1939

as "my favourite band of all time," believes with some justifica-
tion that Auld and Rich were the "two batteries" who "vitalized"
the band.

George Simon, despite his noted reservations about Buddy
Rich, gave the band's performances a favorable review in *Down
Beat*'s February 1939 issue. Shaw's aggregation, Simon reported,
"really kicks out freely with Seabiscuit gusto when it trots out its
swing" and "can play much prettier stuff than just about any of
the ranking swing outfits." But it was, he suggested, emphatically
a *dance* band—whatever the tempo.

> Shaw, unlike many of the swing bandleaders doesn't hit a lot
> of killer-diller tempos in which it's just a matter of the musi-
> cians or dancers pooping first. Instead, Artie really beats out a
> fine time. He does what few white leaders do and that is beat
> out a number of measures to himself until he hits just the right
> tempo, and then passing it on to his men.[14]

The Shaw band was definitely news. *Down Beat* rushed to
publish breathless capsule biographies of members of his 1939
orchestra. Among the more fanciful entries, trombonist George
Arus was billed as the "Swami of Swing." Trumpeter John Best
was said to be "related to Nathaniel Greene and Nathaniel
Macon of Revolutionary War fame." Tenor saxophonist Tony Pastor was "fond of spaghetti" and also sang "huskily in [the] coloured style." Pianist Bob Kitsis's interests included "concert
music, good literature, Harvard-Yale games and Hedy Lamarr,"
while drummer Buddy Rich—"the fastest drummer among the
whites"—had "been playing the skins since he was a 3 year old."[15]

In its January issue of 1939, *Life* magazine featured a photo-
graphic essay of Shaw's residency at the Hotel Lincoln, in its se-

ries *Life Goes to a Party*. The caption of one photograph of the band playing for evening dancers noted "As the Night Wears On the Jitterbugs Become Considerably Less Sedate." Another *Life* picture showed a young socialite "Trucking on a Table Top While a Waiter Discreetly Removes a Bottle." The rivulets of supporting text contained the intelligence that "twitching jitterbugs" were "a familiar part of American life," but that they were now cavorting to a new master of the swing idiom.

> Like [Benny] Goodman, Shaw leads a solid, exciting band. Like Goodman, he plays the clarinet cleanly and with good taste. His great forte is swinging old popular songs, like *The Indian Love Call*. He is 28, was born in New York City and has played the clarinet for a dozen years. Three years ago he was a respected but little known free lance, [and] played in a jazz concert in New York with a string quartet as accompaniment. Next day he was deluged with jobs. But his unusual group proved a flop. Shaw had to form a more orthodox band. Though he is now growing rich with it he still insists wistfully that his clarinet and strings were a swell combination.

Shaw's burgeoning popularity was attested to by extracts from a poll conducted by *Variety* on the musical tastes of college students. The results, *Life* observed, "show that swing still remains the most popular kind of jazz, although most campuses maintain a nice balance between sweet and swing." Artie Shaw was still "new to most collegians," but his recording of *Begin the Beguine* was popular in the fraternity and sorority houses. A Vassar undergraduate had reported "Artie Shaw is coming fast." A Dartmouth student was quoted as saying, "Shaw is a growing love but is well behind Tommy Dorsey [and] Benny Goodman." An

informant from the conservative campus of Vanderbilt University
in Tennessee announced that his peers liked music they could
dance to—"[Kay] Kyser, Dorsey, [Hal] Kemp. Only the intelli-
gentsia know Shaw well."[16] This last remark would surely have
appealed to the cerebral Shaw.

In forming his several orchestras, Shaw (like Duke Ellington)
would often hire relatively inexperienced players and mold them
to his musical demands. Shaw's great rival, Benny Goodman
(with one notable exception) tended to favor established musicians—like trumpeters Harry James, Ziggy Elman, Jimmy Max-
well, and Cootie Williams—who would immediately fit into the
band's format.[17] Whatever the merits of the Shaw/Goodman hiring policies, the Shaw band of 1939, galvanized by the contributions of Jerry Gray, Buddy Rich, George Auld, and Bernie Privin,
inspired Shaw himself to reach new peaks of technical and musical excellence. "In effect," Schuller writes, "what Artie Shaw
couldn't get out of his first two bands, the second one, at mid-
juncture, *got out of him*."[18] Shaw confirms this opinion in his rec-
ollections of a live engagement played by the band in Pennsylvania:

> Everybody [was] tired, hungry, beat after a long jump on the
> road—and suddenly it happened. It was the best jazz night of
> my life. Most nights, I halfway hoped for rain, so nobody
> would turn up. That way we could play without interference—
> the crowd almost always got between me and the music. But
> on this night everything worked. I had a red-hot first trum-
> pet—and when that first phrase ripped out, everything swung.
> I was at the point where I didn't want to hear the rhythm sec-
> tion. I wanted to do it without leaning on anyone else's beat.

Nobody needed leading. We nearly tore the roof off that place. I could see people looking up out of the sea below, mouths wide open. Funny thing was, later, when the men and I talked it over, nobody had any idea why *then*. What had happened? Next night, we tried again the same way, we blew all right, but the wildness, the savage stuff, had packed up for a while. Funny—maybe a little sad too.[19]

Ironically, the recording and the subsequently revitalized band, which launched Shaw's career as a major figure in American popular music, also brought attendant problems. By his own testimony, Shaw—having craved success (or, as he spells it in his autobiography, "$ucce$$")—now found it difficult to cope with either his fellow musicians or a clamoring public.

The men [in the band] began to treat me more as an employer than as a friend. I soon noticed that they were beginning to behave strangely toward me. I had occasionally gone out to eat with one or another of them when we were out on the road. Now I found a curious reluctance on the part of any one of them to be seen in public with me. Any one of the men who might show any intimacy with me began to be regarded with suspicion by the rest.[20]

Shaw also expressed his dissatisfaction with the excesses of an adoring public—in 1938 he was mobbed by fans on Boston Common, who ripped off his lapels, split his jacket, and badly scratched his face. On another occasion, an excited patron jumped onto the stage of the theater where he was performing, and almost knocked out his front teeth. (This incident elicited from Shaw the laconic comment "John Wilkes Booth, I presume").

The late George Auld remembered the hysteria which surrounded the Shaw band after the release of *Begin the Beguine*.

> In those days, we went into *Begin the Beguine* and played it four times during the night. They were dancing on top of the tables. It was unbelievable. One kid jumped off the front balcony [at the Strand in New York City] and broke a leg. Every time we went into the theme, thirty, forty kids would jump up on the stage. Security would have to come up and put them out. One show we did, as the pit was going down, this little broad jumped on top of the pit, grabbed hold of Artie, and started to dry-hump him! He's holding his clarinet above his head; he don't want to break his reed. Artie was as on fire then, as Sinatra was when he hit it big.[21]

Shaw also began to question the material rewards that were the consequence of such fame and notoriety. As he reflected almost fifty years later: "At the peak of that '38 band, I was making $60,000 a week, which is the equivalent of $600,000 today. It seemed insane. I began to ask myself, 'How can I be getting $60,000 a week when the first clarinet player in the Philharmonic only gets $150 a week?' It began to dawn on me that it was lunacy."[22]

Temperamentally and intellectually unsuited to the life of a teen-age idol, Shaw objected to the police protection and security precautions surrounding his every public appearance. Yet there were repeated claims that swing music—and its latest icon—posed dire threats to American youth. During an appearance of the band at the Fox Theatre in Philadelphia, Shaw was told that there had been such a drop in attendance in the city's schools that a formal complaint against him had been lodged by the Board of Education with the police department.

Shaw also became tired of repeating his growing number of hit recordings. As he later remarked to an interviewer, "How do you do the same tune every night in the same way? How many years can you play *Begin the Beguine* without getting a little vomity? I mean, it's a good tune if you are going to be associated with one tune, but I didn't want that."[23]

At the height of his success, Shaw began to express his dissatisfaction with some of the music masquerading—and being accepted—as Swing. In a magazine article published in 1939, he distinguished carefully between two types of big-band music:

> The first type of swing is that which attempts to blast off the roof. Offensive to most ears and definitely of the musically punch-drunk variety, it is an out-and-out menace. The second classification bears the alliterative titles of "smooth" or "sophisticated" swing. For sheer monotony I don't believe this type of music can be surpassed. There is no attempt at colour or ingenuity. Instrumentalists can almost doze off on the bandstand and it would have no effect on their playing. Swing—and I mean *real* swing—is an idiom designed to make songs more listenable and more danceable than they were in their original form. It is, in sum, the creation and sustenance of a mood. In it, there is blasting, purring, subtlety, obviousness—each in its place. That's what swing means and it will remain only if it continues to explore the possibilities of a composition, whether it is by Bach or Duke Ellington.[24]

The physical strains of an exhausting schedule also took their toll. In addition to recordings, personal appearances, and broadcasts from the Lincoln Hotel, Shaw was musical Master of Ceremonies on the CBS "Melody and Madness" program, sponsored by the makers of Old Gold cigarettes. In the spring of 1939, the

Shaw band opened at the Palomar Ballroom in Hollywood—where, four years earlier, the Goodman orchestra had made its sensational breakthrough. On the opening night, Shaw—who was already suffering from a sore throat—collapsed on the bandstand and was rushed to hospital. Unconscious for five days with a form of leukemia, diagnosed as malignant leucopenia or agranulocytosis, and with a temperature of 105 degrees, he was not expected to live. Confounding medical opinion, he made a slow recovery and remembers that on first gaining consciousness, he saw his friend, singer/actress Judy Garland, sitting at his bedside.

During this California period, Shaw made his first Hollywood movie for MGM—*The Dancing Co-Ed*—and during the shooting stayed at the famous Garden of Allah hotel, where he met F. Scott Fitzgerald, the preeminent novelist of the "Jazz Age." Directed by S. Sylvan Simon (Shaw later remarked that "S stood for 'Simple'") the film—a mindless vehicle for its rising starlet, Lana Turner, who later briefly became Mrs. Shaw—was a campus "comedy" which capitalized on the swing phenomenon then sweeping the country. It features a great deal of jitterbugging, a jam session in a plane, and Artie Shaw and his orchestra playing *Nightmare, Non-Stop Flight, I've Got a Feeling You're Fooling, Traffic Jam, Lady Be Good, Jungle Drums*, and *Stars and Stripes Forever*.

From the outset, Shaw was unhappy with the demands and requirements of moviemaking. In *Time Is All You've Got*, he states that the director was "totally insensitive," and Shaw the *actor* resolutely refused to deliver a line of dialogue beginning "Hepcats and alligators" because "I said, 'I don't *talk* that way. I've got a radio programme sponsored by Old Gold that's heard by 20 or 30 million people a week.'" Sylvan retorted that "The audience you play for is infinitesimal compared with the one that's gonna see this movie." Shaw responded scathingly, "You hope," and tried to buy his way out of the film, but the producers refused the offer. "From then on in," Shaw remembered, "if I didn't speak the exact lines in the script, I wasn't gonna get to talk. We ended up with a movie where I say nothin' but 'Yeah, but . . .' Too stupid for words." On another occasion, Shaw said of *The Dancing Co-Ed*: "Talk about abortions—boy, that was long before they were legal."[25] Lana Turner remembered that during the filming of *The Dancing Co-ed,* Shaw "never missed a chance to complain that it was beneath him to appear in a Hollywood movie. The crew plotted to drop an arc light on his head."[26]

Back in New York City, where the band commenced a long engagement at the Cafe Rouge of the Hotel Pennsylvania, Shaw received a great deal of publicity for his stinging comments on the mindlessness of the jitterbugging generation. In an interview with *New York Post* columnist Michael Mok, Shaw had announced "I hate the music business. I'm not interested in giving people what they want. I'm interested in making music." Warming to this theme, he added: "Autograph hunters? The hell with them. They aren't listening—only gawking. My friends, my advisors tell me that I'm a damned fool. 'Look here,' they shout at me. 'You can't do that. These people made you.' You want to know my answer? I tell them that if I was made by a bunch of morons, that's just too bad."

Benny Goodman—also recoiling from the excesses of "hoodlum jitterbugs" and the coarsening of Swing—issued a similar (but less robust) critique in *Collier's* magazine in February 1939:

"We learned to play against hell and high water. We played loud when we should have played soft and played louder when we normally would have played loud. Musical subtlety, just coming to life, went out of the window and the era of Sandblast Swing came in."[27]

Following complaints from outraged fans, Old Gold cancelled its sponsorship of Shaw's radio show. Talking to George T. Simon, shortly after the *Post* revelations, Shaw confirmed and amplified his attitudes, "I don't like jitterbugs. I don't like the business angles connected with music. I can't see autograph hunters. I thought the Old Gold programme was lousy for my music." He also told Simon:

> Frankly, I'm unhappy about the music business. Maybe I don't belong in it. I like the music—love it and live it, in fact—but for me the business part plain stinks. Two years ago we used to love playing; we made up tunes on the stand. Now it's all business. I'm a musician, not a businessman. If I wanted to go into business, I'd enter Wall Street and at least keep regular hours.[28]

In fact, during his six-week convalescence in California, Shaw had already resolved to quit the "music business." The causes were long-standing: his frequently declared dissatisfaction with the state of the entertainment industry in which he was an increasingly unwilling participant, the intrusions on his private life, and his conviction that commercial catering to popular taste relied on the lowest common denominator. The occasion for his announced—but short-lived—retirement came on November 18, 1939, at the Pennsylvania Hotel's Cafe Rouge after "a slight unpleasantness with some idiot on the floor in front of the band, who was evidently trying to impress his partner by using me as a focal point of his witticisms." Eschewing violence against the offending patron, Shaw relates, "I walked off the bandstand, went up to my room, called my lawyer and told him I was leaving."

Buddy Rich, in conversation with Mel Tormé in 1975, remembered that on opening night at the Cafe Rouge, Shaw "left during the first set. He didn't show up on the bandstand. 'Where's Artie?' The room was packed. I sat down behind the drums and waited. We all started looking around at each other. Everybody in the brass section looking at me. I'm looking at them. Finally after about five minutes of waiting, Tony Pastor got up in front of the band and called a set. Artie never came back. We came in the next night. Artie was not there."[29]

Over the objections of his advisors—who correctly pointed out that he was under contract to RCA—Shaw insisted that he was departing immediately for a long vacation, and that the band and its responsibilities were theirs. He left that night, and drove out of New York City, with no idea of his destination: "I remember coming out on the Jersey end of the Holland Tunnel and suddenly realizing I was out from under all that misery and idiocy I'd been buried in for so long."[30]

Shaw's precipitate action, widely reported in the press, drew from the *New York Times* the gnomic reflection that:

Any commentary that might occur to us would be lost in our sense of admiration at the Shakespearean sweep of Mr. Shaw's exodus: the kind of spectacularly irreverent farewell to his work and former associates that even the timidest soul must occasionally dream of, a beautifully incautious burning of all his bridges behind him.[31]

Down Beat magazine also came to Shaw's defense, citing his "tough publicity breaks" following his "very human preference to be a good musician instead of a good businessman." In fact, he was to be praised for his "courage and honesty," which deserved the respect of "businessmen and promoters for the musician trying to be a better musician."[32]

More than thirty years after this signal event, Shaw was prepared to concede that he had acted hastily:

> I just got up and walked away in the middle of the night; leaving all the debris behind and letting anyone who wanted to scrabble for what was left. What I *really* should have done would have been to present my agents and lawyers with a viable set of alternatives. As it was, I kept saying "I need a vacation!"[33]

George T. Simon—the recipient of this confession—has summarized the myriad responsibilities of bandleaders, who were required

> to deal daily and directly—and not only on a musical but also on a personal basis—with their musicians, their vocalists and their arrangers, directing and supervising and bearing the responsibilities of each of these groups. But that wasn't all. Their survival also depended a great deal on how well they dealt with all kinds of people outside their bands—with personal managers, booking agents, ballroom, night-club and hotel-room operators, with head waiters and waiters and busboys, with bus

drivers, with band boys, with the press, with publicity men, with music publishers, with all the various people from the radio stations and from the record companies, and, of course, at all times, with the ever-present, ever-pressuring public. No wonder Artie Shaw ran away to Mexico![34]

Writing in the *Melody Maker* in December 1938, Leonard Feather attempted to explain (and exonerate) Shaw's flight to his British fans. Reminding them that Shaw had, on several occasions, threatened to quit the music business, Feather suggested that he was "a sincere musician, with an extremely sensitive nature, and unaffected personality," emotionally unsuited to the demands and rigors of the commercial world of swing and its grotesque portrayal by Hollywood. Citing Shaw's controversial *New York Post* interview, Feather commented:

> To Artie Shaw, fame, money, the adulation of his thousands of admirers meant nothing, especially if it means he has to hypocritically smile at them, sign autographs [and] be a movie actor when he isn't one. Unfortunately he was unable to do either without doing it for the listening public, who would pay to make it financially possible for Artie Shaw to continue doing those things he wanted to do.

Feather concluded his apologia with the assurance that Shaw had not given upon the idea of being a band leader. Rather, he no longer wanted to lead a *swing* band in the conventional sense of that term, and still "considered his original band (which featured strings prominently) of far more value musically than the orthodox combination of which he has just unburdened himself."[35]

The subject of these reflections was spending his time relaxing and enjoying the local scene in Acapulco, where he "swam, fished, lay in the sun, loafed around [and] did absolutely nothing I didn't feel like doing."[36] On his return to the United States, Shaw wrote a long article for the *Saturday Evening Post* in which he offered further reflections on the sterility of the current music scene:

> Anyone can lead a dance band. At least, anyone could lead many of today's name bands. None of them need leaders—and very few have them. The average band leader is only a front, a window dressing. If he has capable musicians behind him and imaginative arrangers behind the musicians, it doesn't matter whether he's on or off the platform—the music will sound the same.

There were, of course, honorable exceptions, and the most honorable was Duke Ellington.

> Jazz means more to him than a cacophony of blasting brasses or the saccharin strains of a corny ballad. I wish every amateur musician could sit in on an Ellington rehearsal. Music is made on the spur of the moment, *ad lib*. Phrasing is born of inspiration. The man lives it.

Given his repeated attacks on the "commercialism" of the big-band industry, and his unhappy experiences with sponsors, managers, and philistine jitterbugs, Shaw's conclusion was quaintly illogical.

> I should never have been a success or made money in the music business. Having broken every rule and regulation for

subservience, having fed the public songs everyone was convinced the public didn't want to hear, I should have been out in the cold a long time ago. Some people in the business think I'm either cracked or a poseur. They refuse to believe that, with me, music is first.[37]

Shaw now announced his intention of forming a sixty-five piece orchestra, but was still under contract to RCA Victor for six more recording sessions. On March 3, 1940, with a band composed largely of Hollywood studio musicians, Shaw produced the delightful *Frenesi*—based on what he believed was a folk tune that he had heard during his stay in Mexico—and arranged by the African-American composer William Grant Still. With its cheerful and sprightly scoring for strings, and a melodic trumpet solo by Manny Klein, *Frenesi* was an immediate success—despite having already been recorded by Xavier Cugat—and enjoyed huge sales and generous air time.

Schuller damns *Frenesi* with faint praise as being "only minimally and sporadically related to anything one could call jazz," despite superbly executed and melodic solos by trumpeter Manny Klein and horn player Jack Cave. Again, Shaw's idea of hiring William Grant Still "to arrange all six tunes on that first 1940 date, was perhaps a noble and generous thought but musically a mistake. Still's arrangements—*Frenesi* was by far the best—were mostly trite, formless, eclectic in the extreme—and, incidentally, quite jazz-less."[38]

If *Frenesi* was not "jazz," it certainly was not "folk" music. Shaw later confessed that "I thought it was a folk song. That little error cost me approximately half a million dollars. Under the usual system, I could have made a deal with the composer [Alberto Dominguez] for 50 per cent of the take in return for recording the tune. As it was, he got the money."[39] The other titles recorded on the same day as *Frenesi* were *Adios, Marquita Linda* (another tune Shaw had heard in Mexico), and *Gloomy Sunday* (with a vocal by Pauline Byrne). Richard Sudhalter writes that William Grant Still's arrangement of *Gloomy Sunday*—with its unusual instrumental combinations and timbres—"turns the dirge-like Hungarian song into a tone poem, a multi-hued tapestry." Also notable were *My Fantasy, Don't Fall Asleep*, and an orchestration of Edward MacDowell's piano piece, *A Deserted Farm*, unissued until 1978. Schuller aptly comments on this last title that: "It would have been better left in the Victor vaults, for in Still's turgid transcription it sounds like a fourth-rate out-of-tune symphony orchestra, the naively touching romanticism of the piano original mired in a morass of sentimentality."[40] But *Down Beat* praised these new recordings by "a beautiful and melodic-sounding group, with special arrangements by Artie and William Grant Still, the noted Negro composer and arranger."[41]

The success of *Frenesi* prompted Shaw to organize a new band which, with several changes of personnel, lasted until March 1941. It included a string section and several eminent jazz players: trumpeter Billy Butterfield, trombonists Jack Jenney and Vernon Brown, tenor saxophonist Jerry Jerome, pianist Johnny Guarnieri, and drummer Nick Fatool. Their recording of *Stardust*, arranged by Lennie Hayton, with solos by Butterfield, Shaw, and Jenney, and sensitive scoring for the string section, was a major hit. Shaw credits Lennie Hayton with much of the success of *Stardust*.

> I wrote a simple sketch for *Stardust* with the basic framework, and then Lennie Hayton orchestrated it. I would often write

out the lead for most of our songs and let others finish it and give them credit. I differed with Benny Goodman about that. He'd fire people if they received more applause than him, but I figured that if they are playing well, it makes my band sound better; besides, my name is still up in front.[42]

Buddy DeFranco, who absorbed the advanced innovations of be-bop, and transposed them to the clarinet, informed Whitney Balliett in 1982 that "it's arrogant to destroy a melody," and advised him to "listen to Artie Shaw's solo on his recording of *Star Dust*. It's the greatest clarinet solo of all time."[43] Gunther Schuller recalls being on tour in 1943 as a young horn player "and hearing Shaw's *Star Dust* on every jukebox in every restaurant— *three years* after the record was issued." For Schuller, the high point of *Stardust* was Jenney's remarkable trombone solo, which was

considered in its day, for all its romantic cast, a major breakthrough statement, both in technical and expressive terms. The (for the time) extraordinary octave leap to high F was admired far and wide by musicians and sophisticated audiences, not only for the ease with which Jenney managed the deed, but for his elegance and sensitivity of phrasing. Few trombonists have ventured into that uppermost range of the instrument [and] never head-on in such a difficult, dare-devil octave leap. Jenney's rich, full-bodied sound added to the emotional appeal of the passage.

Shaw has confirmed Schuller's memory of the sensational impact of *Stardust*.

Harry Myerson, an A & R man, called me one day [and] said, "We want to do *Stardust*, two sides with our biggest-selling artists—you and Tommy Dorsey. Two versions, same record. No A & B sides. How does that strike you?" I said, "Fine," and we went into the studio to make the record of *Stardust*. It worked on the first take. I said, "Fellas, let's go home because it ain't gonna get any better," and we left. About a week later, I called Harry. I said, "What happened?" He said, "Well, Tommy came in and he wanted to hear what you did. The guys were sitting in the studio waiting to go, and they put on your record, and Tommy says, "I ain't getting on the back of that." So that was the end of that. My record came out, and Tommy lost on the sale of about 16 million records.[44]

From this new band, Shaw formed the first of several versions of his "Gramercy Five"—actually groups ranging from quintets to septets, but all listed as "Artie Shaw and His Gramercy Five." Named after a New York City telephone exchange, Shaw's original and subsequent Gramercy Fives were his rather belated response to the existence of small groups formed by other bandleaders out of their orchestras: Benny Goodman's Trio, Quartet, and Sextet, Tommy Dorsey's Clambake Seven, Woody Herman's Woodchoppers, Bob Crosby's Bob Cats, and the classic small-group studio recordings of the 1930s by Duke Ellington, Lionel Hampton, Teddy Wilson, and John Kirby. Whitney Balliett suggests that

In the late thirties, big bands, which had been prevalent in American popular music for over a decade, remembered that they had grown out of small bands, and, as a salute to their origins, many of them formed small bands-within-bands. All these, lest they grow presumptuous, were given rib-tickling names. Tommy Dorsey and his Clambake Seven, Chick Webb and his Little Chicks, Artie Shaw and his Gramercy Five, Bob Crosby and his Bobcats, Woody Herman and his Woodchoppers'[45]

More specifically, Shaw's use of the harpsichord (played by Johnny Guarnieri) in his first Gramercy Five may have been directly prompted by Benny Goodman's successful appearances and recordings with Lionel Hampton on vibraphone, as a member of the Benny Goodman Quartet.[46] Alyn Shipton places the Gramercy Five somewhere between the Dorsey (Dixieland) and Goodman (Swing) small units.

> Its most distinctive element was that pianist Johnny Guarnieri played harpsichord, which gave the rhythm a jangly, staccato structure, although his carefully picked out right-hand solo lines sounded like a rather strange and stilted breed of acoustic guitar, contrasting with the fluency and smoothness of Al Hendrickson's genuine electric guitar.[47]

Unlike Goodman, who went outside his regular band to form his first Trio and Quartet, Shaw was able to draw on the members of his current orchestra: Billy Butterfield (trumpet), Johnny Guarnieri (harpsichord), Al Hendrickson (guitar), Jud DeNaut (bass), and Nick Fatool (drums). John P. Callanan writes:

> Shaw put his newly-formed Gramercy Five through its paces in his Hollywood home on Summit Ridge Drive, rehearsing only head arrangements of both original and standard material. Nothing was committed to paper, which partly accounts for

the loose feel displayed by the group. Apart from the skilfully executed ensemble passages, everything played by these musicians was improvised.[48]

The Gramercy Five made its first studio recordings in Hollywood on September 3, 1940: *Special Delivery Stomp, Summit Ridge Drive* (the biggest seller of all the Gramercy Five recordings), *Keepin' Myself for You,* and *Cross Your Heart.* These were followed two months later by four more titles: *Dr. Livingstone, I Presume* (on which Shaw plays an amusing cadenza in the Jewish *frahlich* style, popularized by trumpeter Ziggy Elman on Benny Goodman's recording of *Bei Mir Bist Du Schon*), *My Blue Heaven, Smoke Gets in Your Eyes,* and *When the Quail Come Back to San Quentin.* Commenting on his 1954 Gramercy Five version of the last title, Shaw admits that it was a play on the demotic phrase "San Quentin Quail," meaning a sexually attractive girl, under the legal age of consent, or "jail bait"—as in the phrase "a quail who could put a male in San Quentin prison." When Shaw was pestered by a song-plugger to record the maudlin *When the Swallows Come Back to Capistrano,* he eventually "obliged" with the scatological title.

Shortly before his death in 1988, trumpeter Billy Butterfield recalled his tenure with the Gramercy Five units:

It was a *marvellous* little band. We rehearsed a lot, we worked on it, and every number that we did was well prepared long before we did it. Artie was a perfectionist, like Benny Goodman. Both of them were perfectionists. Artie was a really good guy to work for. He treated you very well. He told me one time "You know, to be a player you gotta practice and live with the horn at all times." And [then] he didn't want to be that strict of a player any more, and rather than trying to do it halfway, he just said, "I'll do it no way," and he became a writer.[49]

During the first Gramercy Five period, Shaw and his orchestra were also filming the Paramount movie *Second Chorus* (released in 1940) in Hollywood. Directed by H. C. Potter, the film provided Shaw with a featured and semi-autobiographical role. Initially, at least, he was enthusiastic about the script, written by his friend, Frank Cavett.

> It was a serious story about a young, second-generation Irish kid, son of an immigrant Irishman who settled out West and built himself a big contracting business. He wanted his son to have the advantages he didn't, and sent him to college. Kid went to Yale, where Frank had gone and played in the Yale college band where I met him when I was a little kid. So this trumpet player went to Yale and while he was there he got struck by the beginnings of jazz and became a sort of a young-man-with-a-horn kind of thing. And when he went home from college, he told his father he had no intention of taking over the old contracting business but wanted to be a musician. Father being horrified, rather than break the old man's heart, the kid finally agreed he would give it a year or so, and try working in the contracting business. After two or three years he said to his father, "Look, I'm sorry but I can't do it. I've gotta get back." So he went to New York and tried to get back in the music business, and in those two or three years that had gone past him, he was no longer in. It was meant to be a kind of sad story and comment on what jazz was as a growing, evolving art form. In those days, people thought if you were playing jazz, you were stepping down. And in the film, we had the intention

of showing that if you wanted to play jazz, you had to step way up.[50]

John Garfield was to have played the part of the young trumpet player, but Boris Morros, the producer, opted for Fred Astaire, together with Burgess Meredith and Paulette Goddard, in what became a travesty of the original script. *New Yorker* film critic Pauline Kael provides a succinct summary of the plot and performances of *Second Chorus*—one of Fred Astaire's most dismal musicals:

> At the time, it was generally considered his worst picture, and Astaire himself later concurred in the judgement. He plays an overage undergraduate—a swing bandleader who keeps flunking his exams so that he can stay in college. The band is actually Artie Shaw's considerably augmented. Astaire's romantic and tap partner is Paulette Goddard, who manages the band. The funnymen, Charles Butterworth and Jimmy Conlin, don't compensate for the scarcity of good numbers.[51]

Shaw is seen with his band, playing several titles, including *Dig It, Sweet Sue,* and *Poor Mr. Chisholm.* Nick Fatool is prominently displayed and heard on drums, Bobby Hackett ghosts the trumpet playing of Astaire, and Billy Butterfield that of Meredith. In the most interesting musical sequence, Shaw performs a *Swing Concerto*—later expanded and recorded as *Concerto for Clarinet*—and remembered:

> There was a sequence in it [*Second Chorus*] where we were playing a concert and I wrote a piece for Fred [Astaire], who was going to do a dancing/conducting thing—which was so

cornball but we had to do it. By then we were stuck and that
was the last movie I had anything to do with—that is, as a performer. So during the concert, there was a sequence in which
my band had to play something; it was obligatory. There I was
in the picture. So I wrote a thing called *Concerto for Clarinet*.
It was a framework. I didn't really write anything. I just dic-
tated a frame. Part of it was blues; part of it was not.[52]

The new Shaw orchestra began to attract attention, and was
heard on the Burns and Allen radio show, performing such numbers as *Jungle Drums*, *Nobody Knows the Trouble I've Seen*, and
Diga Diga Doo. Studio recordings by the band at this time included *Who's Excited? Chantez les Bas*, *Stardust*, and, most fa-
mously, *Concerto for Clarinet*, Parts 1 and 2, which has elicited
differing critical and descriptive comments. Albert McCarthy
writes:

> Shaw states the theme over the strings before the full ensem-
> ble plays a bridge to [Johnny] Guarnieri's boogie-style solo,
> after which Shaw, [Jerry] Jerome, [Vernon] Brown and [Billy]
> Butterfield are featured. The first part closes with Shaw ini-
> tially in the high register against the full ensemble, scaling
> down to a quieter passage by him against the strings. The sec-
> ond part is virtually all Shaw, much of the time playing over
> an insistent tom-tom beat by Nick Fatool; he concludes with
> a coda in the high register. It is a very impressive virtuoso per-
> formance, and one that led to a number of poor imitations dur-
> ing [the] war years.[53]

On the other hand, Gunther Schuller dismisses *Concerto for
Clarinet* as "a pastiche thrown together out of some boogie-woo-

gie blues, clarinet-over-tom-tom interludes, a commonplace riff towards the end, all encased in opening and closing virtuoso cadenzas from the leader's clarinet."[54] McCarthy is closer to the mark. The classic nine-minute-and-thirty-two-second performance of *Concerto for Clarinet* is an exciting and memorable demonstration of Shaw's ability to improvise on blues changes, without becoming either repetitive or trite.

In March 1941, Shaw brought some members of the band that now included trombonist-arranger Ray Conniff (who, in the 1950s was to achieve fame with his instrumental and vocal arrangements of light popular music) to New York, where they recorded four instrumental titles at the Victor studios: If *I Had You, It Had to Be You, Georgia,* and *Why Shouldn't I.*

Shaw again disbanded, and before organizing a new orchestra, assembled an unusual group, comprising three major African-American musicians—Henry "Red" Allen (trumpet), Benny Carter (alto), and J. C. Higginbotham (trombone)—together with a rhythm section of Sonny White (piano), Jimmy Shirley (guitar), Billy Taylor (bass), and Shep Shepard (drums), plus thirteen strings—including harpist Laura Newell—to record two titles with vocalist Lena Horne: *Love Me a Little* and *Don't Take Your Love from Me.* There were also instrumental versions of *I'm Confessin' That I Love You* and *Beyond the Blue Horizon.*

In the autumn of 1941, Shaw formed another band, which featured (in addition to a string section) Conniff and Jack Jenney (trombones), George Auld (tenor), Dave Tough (drums), and the Texan-born black trumpeter Oran "Hot Lips" Page, who is the soloist and singer on several fine recordings, including *Blues in the Night, Take Your Shoes Off, Baby,* and *St. James Infirmary.*

One of the great jazz trumpet players—although considerably less talented than his idol, Louis Armstrong—Page was a master of the plunger mute, and can be heard to good effect in many of his solo spots with Shaw (1941–1942). When the General Artists Corporation demanded that he drop Page from a tour of the Southern States in 1941—unless he sat no closer than fifteen feet to the nearest (white) member of the band—Shaw cancelled thirty-two Southern engagements. The *Daily Worker* promptly hailed Shaw for his stand against "Jim Crow in popular music circles."[55]

Shaw expressed great hopes for his new aggregation, which received a generally favorable notice by George Frazier in *Down Beat*:

> Artie Shaw's new band represents nothing either radical or deeply significant, but it is one of the most competent bands anywhere. It is big (32 pieces), beautifully drilled, and musical all over the place. The star of Artie's band is Dave Tough. His drumming is nothing short of stupendous. There is never any exhibitionism to anything that Tough does, never any of the juvenile delinquency of Buddy Rich's playing, for example— just enormous competence, impeccable taste, and one of the most miraculous beats in jazz.

The praise for Tough was decidedly prescient, since his superb drumming was crucial both to the fire and the success of Woody Herman's wonderful First Herd.

Shaw, Frazier asserted, had collected "some of the most glowing talents in the profession and moulded them into something, if not unique, at least immensely satisfying." The string section was "anything but disagreeable," and blended well with the rest of the band. Among the band's "first-rate" soloists, Frazier listed Max Kaminsky and Lips Page, Jack Jenney and Ray Conniff, and altoist Les Robinson. Shaw himself was playing superbly and appeared "to be a much changed guy personally. The men enjoy working for him and are grateful for the fact that he shows no disposition to tell them how to play their instruments."[56]

On record and on tour, Shaw's final pre-war band played essentially jazz-inflected dance music. George T. Simon characterizes the 1941 Shaw orchestra as "simply a fine dance band, with strings and an ability to play exceptionally good jazz and ballads," and one which would "have caused more of a general furore had it lasted long enough."[57]

Shaw himself was continually experimenting with and adding to the band's library. He hired various arrangers—Bill Challis, Lennie Hayton, Margie Gibson, and Fred Norman—all of who attempted to integrate the string section effectively with the orchestra. Shaw also commissioned Paul Jordan to write classically based pieces for the band. Born in Chicago in 1916—and mistakenly identified in some accounts as an African-American—Jordan produced two interesting compositions, *Evensong* and *Suite No. 8*, for Shaw. Schuller devotes four pages to an in-depth musical analysis of these two pieces and writes: "*Evensong* is a little gem. Essentially an 'Aria' for clarinet and orchestra, serene in its twilight mood, it affords Shaw an excellent opportunity to display his supremely beautiful tone." Schuller identifies Hot Lips Page as the trumpet soloist in *Suite No. 8*, and judges Shaw's solo as displaying "fine swing energy" but also, in deference to Jordan's framework, confining himself "to a relatively controlled improvisation." Schuller also suggests persuasively that these two pieces "stand in relation to Shaw's orchestra much as Ralph Burns's *Summer Sequence* stands to Woody Herman's 1945 Herd," while Shaw's relationship with Jordan anticipates that of the "Progressive" bandleader Stan Kenton with Bob Graettinger.[58]

Sixteen days before Shaw recorded Jordan's two compositions, the Japanese (on December 7, 1941), attacked the American fleet at Pearl Harbor, and the United States formally declared war on the Axis powers. On what Franklin D. Roosevelt termed a "day that will live in infamy," the Shaw band was appearing at the Metropole Theater in Providence, Rhode Island. Asked by the manager to announce to service personnel in the audience that they had to report to their bases immediately, Shaw cancelled the remainder of the performance. In retrospect, Shaw believed that "my career as a serious dedicated player of a musical instrument ended in 1941, when the war started. With the whole world in flames, playing *Stardust* seemed pretty pointless."

Ironically, given Shaw's expressed disenchantment with the role of civilian bandleader in a time of national crisis, the war years revitalized the popularity of big bands on the home front, and provided welcome employment opportunities for those musicians who did not serve in the armed forces. By 1941, the burgeoning war industries and full employment brought America out of the Depression years, and stimulated the entertainment industry. But the artificial stimulation of a wartime economy also "temporarily disguised the structural problems in the music industry and postponed the inevitable collapse of the Swing Era until shortly after the troops returned home in 1945."[59]

Before enlisting in the armed forces, Shaw went to California and returned to the East Coast with Elizabeth Kern, daughter of Jerome Kern, and shortly to become Mrs. Shaw. After playing a final engagement in Detroit, Shaw was driven by his new wife to 90 Church Street in New York City, where he was formally inducted into the United States Navy.

NOTES

1. Ross Firestone, *Swing, Swing, Swing*, 232.

2. Artie Shaw, Taped Interview with Joe Thompson, Newbury Park, November 20, 1979, in possession of author.

3. Owen Peterson, "Artie Shaw," *Jazz Journal*, 22 (Sept. 1969), 16. Peterson's unabashed admiration for Miller's *American Patrol* is the more remarkable since that plodding opus resolutely refuses to swing. He also appears to be singularly unaware of (or immune to) the sheer *sexiness* of Shaw's *Begin the Beguine*. In the Introduction to his collection of jazz record reviews, originally published in the *Daily Telegraph*, Philip Larkin imagines his readers (of 1968) as "sullen fleshy inarticulate men, stockbrokers, sellers of goods, living in 30-year-old detached houses among the golf courses of Outer London, husbands of ageing and bitter wives they first seduced to Artie Shaw's *Begin the Beguine*." *All What Jazz: A Record Diary 1961–68* (London: Faber and Faber, 1970), 28.

4. Schuller, *The Swing Era*, 698.

5. Simon, *The Big Bands*, 415–16.

6. *The Swing Era*, 700.

7. Gene Lees, *Meet Me at Jim & Andy's: Jazz Musicians and Their World* (New York and Oxford: Oxford University Press, 1988), 63.

8. *Swing, Swing, Swing*, 232. Schuller comments that "Shaw's greatest success, both popular and critical, came at the very time (mid-

1939), when Goodman had slipped down from the high crest of his initial popularity, reaching a temporary nadir, and in fact disbanding for a while, but reorganizing a few months later with an entirely new band." *The Swing Era*, 701.

9. Whitney Balliett, *Barney, Bradley, and Max: 16 Portraits in Jazz* (New York & Oxford: Oxford University Press, 1989), 191.

10. Blandford, *Artie Shaw*, 61.

11. Scott Yanow, "Profile: Artie Shaw," *Jazziz*, 9 (July 1992), 102. *The Big Bands*, 548. Whitney Balliett, *Goodbyes and Other Messages: A Journal of Jazz 1981–1990* (New York & Oxford: Oxford University Press, 1991), 196.

12. Mel Tormé, *Traps The Drum Wonder: The Life of Buddy Rich* (Edinburgh and London: Mainstream Publishing, 1991), 44. Schuller has no doubts on this score: "Rich brought to the Shaw band the musical energy and drive that he had gleaned from Chick Webb, Jo Jones, Sid Catlett, and other major black big-band drummers. This elemental force in turn stimulated Shaw to ever greater heights, not only as a soloist but even as an arranger." *The Swing Era*, 701.

13. After leaving Shaw, Privin became a member of Charlie Barnet's band and then joined Glenn Miller's Army Air Force band in 1943. Privin found Miller's strict discipline hard to accept. On one occasion, Miller ordered all band members wearing moustaches to shave them off—to the great detriment of Privin's embouchure. He rejoined Goodman after being discharged and then spent twenty-two years as a staff musician for CBS.

14. George T. Simon, *Simon Says*, 122–26.

Seabiscuit was a champion racehorse of the 1930s. In a later estimate, Simon conceded that "Buddy did soon settle into a tremendous groove and the Shaw band began to swing as it never had with any of its previous drummers." In his 1939 review, Simon also faulted the saxophone section which was "inclined to be sloppy, not so much in the attacking as in the holding of notes."

15. Blandford, 55–58. *Passim*.

16. *Life*, Vol.6 (January 23, 1939), 60–62.

17. The great exception is electric guitarist Charlie Christian, who was introduced to—and imposed on—an initially reluctant Goodman

by John Hammond. See John Hammond with Irving Townsend, *John Hammond on Record* (Harmondsworth, Middlesex: Penguin Books, 1981), 223–28, 232–33. Philip Larkin relates: "When critic John Hammond smuggled Charlie Christian through the kitchen and on to the stand of the Victor Hugo in Los Angeles in August, 1939, he was unwittingly setting one of those legendary scenes that jazz abounds in. The leader, Benny Goodman, was having dinner. Arriving back, he was furious to see this 20-year-old gangling, unpolished Negro planted, amplifier and all, among the Sextet: he might have ordered him out. Instead, he called for *Rose Room*. It was a wise decision. That was the longest *Rose Room* Benny ever played, forty-five minutes of trading new, exciting phrases with a jazz stylist of complete originality. Christian's long-running single-note phrases and seemingly inexhaustible vocabulary of riffs were utterly contemporary—even, perhaps, a hint of things to come. At the end of *Rose Room* the Goodman band had a new guitarist." "Goodman's Guitar Man," All *What Jazz*, 170–71.

18. *The Swing Era*, 701.

19. Taylor, "Middle-Aged Man Without a Horn," 63.

20. *The Trouble With Cinderella*, 339.

21. *Traps The Drum Wonder*, 44.

22. Joe Smith, *Off the Record: An Oral History of Popular Music*, edited by Mitchell Fink (London: Sidgwick and Jackson, 1989), 1.

23. *Ibid*. In the same vein, Shaw asked rhetorically: "Do you know how boring it is to start a show with *'S Wonderful* and end it with *Concerto for Clarinet?* Whenever I changed a tune, the manager would come running and say, 'Dammit, don't do that. Those kids will be here all day.' How could you live with that?" *Ibid*. Philip Larkin recognizes and identifies this problem. "The golden rule in any art is: once you have made your name, keep in there punching. For the public is not so much endlessly gullible as endlessly hopeful: after twenty years, after forty years even, it still half-expects your next book or film or play to reproduce that first fine careless rapture, however clearly you have demonstrated that whatever talent you once possessed has long since degenerated into repetition, platitude or frivolity. A commonplace in the more established arts, it is true of jazz also." "Great Expectations," *All What Jazz*, 239.

24. Bruce Crowther and Mike Pinfold, *The Big Band Years* (London: David & Charles, 1988), 65.

25. Tom Nolan, "Still Cranky After All These Years," *Los Angeles* May 1990, 111; *Dialogues in Swing*, 137.

26. Quoted in Sudhalter, *Lost Chords*, 607.

27. Tormé, *Traps The Drum Wonder*, 49–50. Firestone, *Swing, Swing, Swing*, 244.

28. Simon, *Simon Says: The Sights and Sounds of the Swing Era, 1935–1955* (New Rochelle, New York: Arlington House, 1971), 18–19. Shaw told Simon in November 1935 that he was "glad" to have broken with his Old Gold Sponsors: "The show was built all wrong for me. When I auditioned for it, I had a definite musical formula, but it gradually turned into a comedy which didn't do the band any good. Besides, it was on a weak network, thus killing its rating, and the new schedule called for a west coast show at 11 o'clock Saturday nights and I couldn't leave the Penn[sylvania] Hotel for that."

29. *The Trouble With Cinderella*, 351. Tormé comments: "What is fascinating about Buddy's recollection is that he insists that he was still playing with the Shaw band the night Artie left. Yet *Down Beat* reported him joining [Tommy] Dorsey prior to Artie's leave-taking. Since Shaw's actions were of great significance during that period, it would seem unlikely that Rich would forget an episode as startling as Artie walking away from his own men." *Traps The Drum Wonder*, 51. Trumpeter Bernie Privin also retained vivid memories of the Cafe Rouge episode. "An elderly woman asked Shaw to play a tango, maybe it was a rhumba. He said, 'Lady, you're in the wrong room.'" Jerry Gray recalled with some bitterness that Shaw "said not a goddamned thing to us. [He] should have faced us." Guitarist Al Avola reflected that when Shaw walked away "he took the band with him. We tried. We played the same music and it was swinging. But something was missing. He was the band." Chris Albertson, "Artie Shaw," Liner notes to *The Swing Era 1937–1938* (New York: Time-Life Records).

30. *The Trouble With Cinderella*, 353.

31. "Middle-Aged Man Without a Horn," 63. Richard Sudhalter comments wryly on the episode: "No other defection, even at the height

of the Cold War decades later, has been as widely publicized—with so little attempt on the part of its chroniclers to understand what it was, what drove it, and what effect it had." *Lost Chords*, 588. Acapulco may have been Shaw's final destination, but singer Helen Forrest recounts that he was romantically involved with the young Judy Garland—much to her mother's disapproval. Shaw reportedly phoned Garland from Little Rock, Arkansas, requesting her advice. Her reply was that "the world was going nuts because he was among the missing" and suggested that he should "cool it for a while."

Other accounts assert that Betty Grable was the new object of Shaw's attentions at the time of his flight from New York. *Ibid.* 822, Note 35.

32. Chris Albertson. Liner notes to *Begin the Beguine: Artie Shaw and his Orchestra* (RCA CD).

33. *The Big Bands*, 546–7.

34. *Ibid.* 9–10.

35. Blandford, *Artie Shaw*, 227–9.

36. *The Trouble With Cinderella*, 355. One thing that Shaw *did* feel like doing was to rescue—at the cost of a broken kneecap—a young girl swimmer who was in distress.

37. Blandford, *Artie Shaw*, 73, 81.

38. *The Swing Era*, 703.

39. "Middle-Aged Man Without a Horn," 65.

40. *The Swing Era*, 793, n.35.

41. Blandford, *Artie Shaw*, 84.

42. Yanow, "Artie Shaw," 103.

43. *Barney, Bradley, And Max*, 196. Richard Sudhalter endorses—and amplifies—DeFranco's encomium, suggesting that Shaw's *Stardust* solo is "one of the great set-pieces of the jazz canon." Again, like Louis Armstrong's *West End Blues* and Coleman Hawkins's *Body and Soul*, it has convinced many listeners "among them a few clarinetists of stature that the solo can't have been spontaneous [but] must have been worked out very carefully in advance." *Lost Chords*, 592. Alyn Shipton praises Shaw's *Stardust* solo as combining "great tonal beauty with the inevitability of phrasing of the finest jazz soloists, paraphrasing the melody in

a way that created a new structure, but keeping the original firmly in view." *Stardust,* he concedes, "is unquestionably a jazz record, but within it, improvisation is limited to the solos, and like much of Shaw's output it prompts yet another examination of where the definition of jazz should start and finish." *A New History of Jazz,* 349–50.

44. *The Swing Era,* 704. Schuller might also have noted that Jenney's role in this Shaw band presaged that of Bill Harris in Woody Herman's 1945 "Herd"—for example, his plangent solo on *Bijou.*

45. He adds parenthetically: "Mundane old Benny Goodman, mindful that he might one day frequent the conservatory, simply had his trios, quartets, quintets, sextets, and septets." *Night Creature: A Journal of Jazz, 1975–1980* (New York: Oxford University Press, 1981), 33.

46. Guarnieri remembers that "Artie Shaw gave me a lot of liberty. He generated enthusiasm and stimulated my thinking. It led to my playing harpsichord with the Gramercy Five, and I became the first jazzman to jam on a harpsichord. I helped put a lot of those Gramercy Five things together." Arnold Shaw, *52nd Street: The Street of Jazz* (New York: Da Capo Press, 1977), 308. In a 1979 radio interview, Shaw recalled that Guarnieri "had a terrible struggle with it [the harpsichord] at first." He might have added that other notable performers— Meade "Lux" Lewis, Erroll Garner, and Oscar Peterson—failed to transpose their (differing) pianistic techniques entirely successfully to the harpsichord. Two pianists who have made this transition are Hank Jones and Lalo Schifrin.

47. Alyn Shipton, *A New History of Jazz* (London and New York: Continuum, 2001), 350. Shipton asserts that, despite its popularity, "the jazz potential of Shaw's small group was held in check by the gimmick of the harpsichord, and its soloists seldom reached the high levels they managed in other contexts." *Ibid.*

48. Sleeve note to *Artie Shaw: The Complete Gramercy Five Sessions* (RCA CD).

49. W. Royal Stokes, *The Jazz Scene, An Informal History from New Orleans to 1990* (New York: Oxford University Press, 1991), 96.

50. *Dialogues in Swing,* 137–8.

51. Pauline Kael, *5001 Nights at the Movies* (London: Arrow Books, 1987), 518.

52. *Dialogues in Swing*, 138–9.

53. McCarthy, *Big Band Jazz*, 265.

54. Schuller, *The Swing Era*. In a footnote Schuller notes that Shaw's *Concerto for Clarinet* was not only "published and seriously studied by clarinetists and classical musical teachers, [but] is still played nowadays by high-school and college orchestras, trying to show their 'progressiveness.'" 705.

55. Trumpeter Max Kaminsky, who was playing with Shaw at this time, claims to have introduced him to Page, and also relates a possibly apocryphal story. "Lips broke up audiences even in the most segregated sections of the Deep South. One night after the show, a cracker came up to the bandstand and said he thought Lips played so great that he wanted to meet him. After shaking Lips's hand, the southerner said, 'And Ah want you to know this is the first time Ah ever shook the hand of a coloured man.' Lips flashed one of his wide, happy grins and said in his wonderfully pleasing way, 'Well, buddy, it didn't hurt you, now, did it?'" *My Life in Jazz*, 126. Shaw himself recalled: "It was difficult in those days for some of the black people in the band. Hot Lips Page could handle it. He was one of the only ones who could. Lips would say, 'Don't fuck with my living, man.' He was a spark plug." *Off the Record*, 2; *Swingin' the Dream*, 130.

56. Blandford, *Artie Shaw*, 119–20. A later *Down Beat* update reported: "The young man with a stick who once told off America's jitterbugs is now watching them pay cash money to see and hear his new band. Maybe no other leader could have gotten away with it, but Artie appears to be stronger now at the box office than at any time in his stormy career." *Ibid.* 122.

57. *The Big Bands*, 421–2.

58. *The Swing Era*, 707–9. Largely neglected by—or unknown to—most Shaw commentators, *Evensong* and *Suite No. 8* (which, as has been mentioned, is one of Shaw's favorite recordings) are, Schuller suggests, as valid as other "serious compositions" of the swing era: Ralph Burns's *Summer Sequence*, Claude Thornhill's *Snowfall*, or Shaw's own *Concerto for Clarinet*. "Recording and performing Jordan's works," he concludes, "was one of Shaw's most felicitous and generous undertakings, for which we owe him much respect and gratitude." *Ibid.* 710.

59. *Meet Me at Jim and Andy's*, 84–5. *The Birth of Bebop*, 156.

Performing in the Navy, South Pacific, WWII

War and Peace

Artie's personality was still getting people's backs up, but he was having his own troubles too, adjusting to military life and all the Navy red tape and regulations, and he was a natural target in his crisp white chief's uniform, for the bored Navy wives, who all trained their guns on him at every dance we played.

Max Kaminsky

David W. Stowe has suggested that the dynamism and promises associated with swing during the 1930s—"a belief in American exceptionalism, in ethnic pluralism and democratic equality"—were "ideally suited to the collective needs of a nation battling fascism."[1] Swing bandleaders were pressed into the war effort—promoting war bond drives and converting their music "into a semi-official morale-raising medium for military personnel around the world and war industry workers at home."[2]

In 1943, *Down Beat* published a "Band Leaders' Honor Roll" which listed thirty-nine former band leaders in the Army, seventeen in the Navy, three in the Merchant Marine, and two in the Coast Guard.[3] Less than a month after the attack on Pearl Harbor, two hundred swing-band musicians volunteered for United Service Organization (USO) tours of military bases. On Christmas Day 1942, the Coca-Cola company presented forty bands—including those of Duke Ellington, Harry James, and Benny Goodman—in a twelve-hour broadcast over 142 American radio stations. Most important for the dissemination of jazz and swing music to American military audiences was the Army's "V Disc" program, established in late 1943 by the Special Services Division. Manufactured by engineers and producers from RCA Victor and Columbia, the twelve-inch discs—studio and "live" recordings, air checks, and film scores—featured such jazz notables as Louis Armstrong, Roy Eldridge, Duke Ellington, Benny Goodman, Coleman Hawkins, Billie Holiday, Art Tatum, and Fats Waller. Broadcast through the American Expeditionary Service, V Discs were also heard by radio listeners in Europe, and gained new (and often literally captive) audiences for swing music.[4]

Artie Shaw's two great clarinet-playing rivals did not see active service. Because of a back condition, Benny Goodman was classified as 4-F by the US Army; Woody Herman was granted exemption because of a hernia. Shaw's first naval duty as an apprentice seaman—after being medically upgraded from category 3-A to 1-A—was aboard a minesweeper, docked at Staten Island, New York. He was then sent to Newport, Rhode Island, to form a band. The prospects were decidedly unpromising. He remembered: "I had two men who could blow good; the rest were terrible. Obviously, our only hope was to shape up with a uniform sound, so I asked the two good men to blow bad. Oddly enough, they refused. I was back where I started as a kid with the Peter Pan Novelty Orchestra."[5] After brief hospitalization for migraine attacks, Shaw went to Washington, D.C., where he persuaded the Secretary of the Navy, James V. Forrestal, to allow him to form a new band to take to the Pacific, and was promoted to the rank of Chief Petty Officer.

Among the drafted or enlisted musicians recruited by Shaw for "Naval Reserve Band 501" (later known as "The Rangers") were trumpeters Max Kaminsky, John Best, and Conrad Gozzo, tenor saxophonist Sam Donahue, pianist Claude Thornhill, and the drummer Dave Tough. The underweight and ailing Dave Tough only passed his medical test when Shaw informed the examining officer, "This is the world's greatest drummer." Shaw had a particular fondness and genuine respect for Tough, who later went on briefly to power the first Woody Herman Herd.

> I first knew Davy in the thirties when he was with Tommy Dorsey, and we'd go up to Harlem to listen to music. He was a sweet man, a gentle man, and not easy to get to. He was shy and reclusive. He had great respect for the English language. He read a lot and I read a lot, so we had that in common. During the Second World War, he was in my Navy band, and we'd manage to get together once in a while and talk. He was an alcoholic, and he always found things to drink. I'd assign a man to him if we had an important concert coming up—say, for the crew of an aircraft carrier—and that man would keep an eye on him all day, so he wouldn't get drunk and fall off the bandstand, which he had done a couple of times. I think he was the most underrated big-band drummer in jazz, and he got a beautiful sound out of his instrument. He tuned his drums, he tried to achieve on them what he heard in his head, as we all do, and I think he came as close as you can get. Whenever I pointed to him for twelve or eight or four bars, he'd smile and shake his head and go on playing rhythm drums.[6]

The selection was completed by the end of November 1942. After preliminary duties in Lower Manhattan, where it was required to perform as a marching band for Navy celebrations and to boost civilian morale, Shaw's Navy band was ordered to Pearl Harbor, where it later joined the battleship *North Carolina* en route to Noumea in the South Pacific. As Max Kaminsky relates, the Shaw band had a poor record for marching:

> We'd rise at 5:30 a.m., my normal bed-time, and march out on the pier to play *Stars and Stripes Forever, Under the Double Eagle Flag, Anchors Aweigh,* and *The Washington Post March* while the poor gobs went through their exercises. Dave [Tough] wasn't strong enough to carry a drum or even the big cymbals, so they gave him a peck horn. It was very funny to see him wrestling with this unfamiliar instrument and trying to get some kind of tone out of it. In fact, we were a horrible excuse for a military band, in spite of the good musicians.[7]

Shaw quickly became disillusioned with life in the US Navy, and spent an inordinate amount of time trying to secure accommodations for his men. "I was," he recalled, "the lowest of the low. The [top] brass considered our mission silly and I heard a lot of 'You're not in Hollywood now.'"[8] For nearly five months, the band stayed in Honolulu, playing at the officers' club, at parties, and giving concerts at camps around the islands. On January 30, 1943, Shaw and the Rangers band played *Begin the Beguine* over the Armed Forces Radio Service (AFRS) as part of *America Salutes the President*—a program celebrating Franklin D. Roosevelt's sixty-first birthday. The Rangers then embarked on a tour of the South Pacific, without Claude Thornhill, whose piano playing had so impressed Admiral Chester W. Nimitz that he was (with Shaw's intercession) allowed to remain in Honolulu and form another Navy band. Shaw's long friendship with the gifted—and guileful—Thornhill had been severely tested when he joined Shaw's Navy band in 1942. Shaw recounts:

I was a CPO, and I was responsible for band discipline, but Claude and I couldn't arrive at a modus vivendi. After all, we had been close a long time, and it wasn't easy being thrust into what amounted to a master-servant relationship. He would miss muster or bed check or rehearsals, and resentment began to build on both sides. He was already a heavy drinker, and that didn't help. He made it known that he wanted his own band, so I talked to Admiral Calhoun, and they gave him one before we left Hawaii for the Pacific Islands. Our relationship was never quite the same, and I didn't see much of Claude after that.[9]

Shaw and the Rangers were overwhelmed by the reception they received from the American forces on their various stops. "We'd set up shop in some eerie tropical setting—palm trees all around, board benches, Navy boys sitting on them or on the ground—and we'd swing into one of the old favourites, really socking it, you could see tears come into their eyes."[10] Max Kaminsky remembered arriving in New Caledonia and being ferried out to the aircraft carrier *Saratoga* to give a concert.

Since it was night the men were gathered on the lower deck, and our entrance alone sent them off into an uproar. We set up the bandstand on the huge aircraft elevator and began playing our theme song *Nightmare* as we descended slowly into the midst of the wildly cheering men. It was like being back at the Paramount again, except that the bandstand there used to rise slowly from the pit, while on the "Saratoga" it descended into the audience. As I sat there looking at these thousands of sailors and feeling the waves of homesickness flow out of them at the sound of the familiar songs, I began to fill up so much that when I stood up to take my solo on the *St. Louis Blues* I blew like a madman. On hearing me let loose, Dave [Tough] started to swing the beat, and when I picked up my plunger and started to growl, those three thousand men went stark raving crazy. Even the fellows in the band were shaken.[11]

But the Rangers' tour of duty also brought physical and mental exhaustion—as well as the constant fear of enemy attack. By the time it reached Australia and New Zealand, Shaw and his musicians had begun to disintegrate. "By then," he writes, "our instruments were being held together by rubber bands and sheer will, having survived any number of air raids and damp spells in fox holes; and the men themselves were for the most part in similarly varying states of dilapidation." In an interview which he later gave to *Metronome*, Shaw, recounting his experiences aboard US Navy ships, exclaimed:

> Was I scared? You bet I was. Conditions were grim. Nearby boats were being torpedoed. You just quake and wonder if it's you or the next guy who got hit. You take your battle station and you do your job.[12]

There were other hazards, including the climate, which destroyed musical instruments. Shaw would be playing a solo "and a pad would drop out of my clarinet." Reeds were scarce, guitar and bass strings kept snapping, "and most of the time there wasn't a PA system, the guys had to blow their brains out to be heard."

Not surprisingly, Shaw himself also snapped. On Guadalcanal, which was being bombed by the Japanese every night, he wandered off into the jungle, suffering from a partial loss of memory. After being picked up by a Navy doctor, he spent some time recovering in a field hospital. By mid-June 1943, he was again leading the Rangers band on various Pacific islands, and again, the response from the troops was overwhelming. Shaw remembered that: "We played many of the old arrangements," and that it was "amazing how the kids out there [were] familiar with the band. They got so excited when we showed up on some god-forsaken island unexpectedly. Some would throw gifts at the band. Most would just sit there and just listen, devouring everything we kicked off." He also recalled hearing his records being played over Radio Tokyo with the accompanying announcement that the band was currently appearing at the St. Francis Hotel in San Francisco: "The idea was to make the Yanks feel homesick."[13]

When he was finally shipped back to San Francisco at the end of 1943, Shaw was photographed down on his knees, kissing the dock. With recurrent migraine headaches, he was medically discharged on February 23, 1944—along with Max Kaminsky and Dave Tough—after spending a period in the Naval Hospital at Oak Knoll, California.[14] The Rangers band—which had won a poll in *Esquire* magazine as the favorite band of the American armed forces—continued under the leadership of Sam Donahue. It became the US Navy Liberation Forces Band, dispensed with the Shaw library, and toured successfully in several European countries.

Divorced from Elizabeth Kern, but greatly attached to their infant son, Stephen, Shaw now underwent a course of psychoanalysis. It was during this period also that he joined several left-wing organizations, some of them with Communist connections, with unforeseen consequences for the future.

In the summer of 1944, *Metronome* announced that Shaw was planning to form a new seventeen-piece band—and one without any strings attached. He had told critic Barry Ulanov that "I don't want to do a lot of theatres. A guy who plays six or seven shows a day in theatres must hate music. I'm critical of my work [and] I'm cursed with serious-mindedness." Ulanov took Shaw's professions of "serious-mindedness" seriously, and characterized him as possessing "a remarkably alert and provocative mind," reflected in his "voracious" reading. The "victim of crude appraisal at least as often as he has been properly praised as a forceful, forward-looking creator," Ulanov predicted that Shaw "despite the questionable limitations and contradictions and aberrations" in his personality could "be counted on the side of what we who look forward to great things in jazz naively call Truth and Beauty."[15]

Shaw formed what was to be the most consistent, innovative, and jazz-oriented of his several orchestras in 1944. Whitney Balliett offers a collective profile of Shaw's various bands:

> The *Begin the Beguine* outfit was tight and springy; it was a snappy Ford coupe. The *Frenesi* band, with its bouffant strings and walk-along tempos, was gentle and subtle, but it had an unmistakable jazz persuasion. It was also a peerless dance band. The 1945 band, with Roy Eldridge, was the closest Shaw came to an out-and-out jazz group. It was a disciplined, swinging, straight-ahead band.[16]

The first titles recorded by the 1944–1945 band for the Victor company on November 23, included *Ac-cent-tchu-ate the Positive*, with a vocal by Imogene Lynn who also sang on the ballad *Let's Take the Long Way Home*. A Jimmy Mundy composition, *Lady Day*, was obviously intended as a tribute to Billie Holiday, while *Jumpin' on the Merry-Go-Round* was later used as a signature tune on the British Armed Forces network in Germany. The rhythm section was Shaw's best, and featured drummer Lou Fromm, bassist Morris Rayman, guitarist Barney Kessel, and pianist Dodo Marmarosa. After Shaw himself, the African-American trumpeter Roy Eldridge was the band's star soloist, and with arrangements by Ray Conniff, Eddie Sauter, Buster Harding, and Bobby Sherwood, they recorded such exhilarating titles as *September Song, Lucky Number, Bedford Drive, 'S Wonderful, Love Walked In, Soon, Tea for Two*, and a special feature for Eldridge, *Little Jazz*.[17]

Shaw himself took great care with the recordings of his 1944–1945 band, and is particularly proud of Eddie Sauter's arrangement of *Summertime*, which also features Roy Eldridge. In *Time Is All You've Got*, he remarks that Eldridge did not want to play the "growl" trumpet chorus, fearing that he would be accused of copying Duke Ellington's expert in that department, Cootie Williams.

Ray Conniff in particular again made an enormous contribution to the band's sound. His arrangements "were characterized by a deep, rich, orchestral sound, finely balanced, set in spicily chromatic harmonies and voicings" as well as by "a structural clarity that consistently avoided congestion and permitted soloists and sections to develop a deep, spacious, laid-back swing."[18] In fact, this was primarily an arranger's band: there were few solo opportunities for Eldridge, and even fewer for Marmarosa, who was already showing enviable talent as a bop-influenced pianist. Fortunately, both Eldridge and Marmarosa were to be featured prominently in a reconstituted Gramercy Five, formed in 1945. It first recordings—*Grabtown Grapple* (named after Ava Gardner's hometown in North Carolina), and *The Sad Sack*—made on January 9, feature Eldridge's abrasive trumpet and Shaw's lucid clarinet. *Scuttlebutt*, recorded on August 2, derives from a slang term that became common during World War II (and may have reflected Shaw's naval experiences). The water bucket or drinking fountain on a ship, in everyday usage it came to mean a rumor or a piece of gossip—because such talk was often indulged in during relaxed conversations around the watering hole: "just scuttlebutt."

The new Gramercy Five was featured wherever the Shaw band appeared, including a broadcast of September 12, 1945, which received a favorable notice in *Metronome*.

> Artie and his lilting clarinet, his star Roy Eldridge, and his band all made a good showing. High spots were the old Shaw favourite *Summit Ridge Drive*, in which Roy and Artie were supported by the same four fine musicians present when the current band was formed: Dodo Marmarosa, Barney Kessel, Lou Fromm, and Morey Rayman. Solos by Marmarosa on piano and Kessel on guitar were tasteful, and Artie himself seemed inspired instead of tired.[19]

Shaw's agents, the General Artists Corporation (GAC), actively promoted his return to band leading, and press handouts stressed his war service. The "handsome ex-Navy veteran" it was claimed, "isn't faced by the problems that face touring bands today" because as a Chief Petty Officer in the Navy he had "led a band in the war-torn areas of the Pacific [and] has played under every handicap imaginable." Aside from numerous torpedo attacks, the Shaw Navy band had "lived through 17 different bombing attacks, usually from high-flying Jap precision bombers trying to score direct hits on U. S. warships which carried Shaw from island to island." Shaw himself was quoted as saying:

> We hitch-hiked everywhere. Sometimes on a large ship, then a smaller one, and sometimes by airplane. We travelled any way we could. We went without sleep. But for everything we went through, it seemed like nothing compared to what the fighting men endured. That pleasure we brought them and the smiles they gave us are worth all the hardships we had gone through. I'd do it again, anytime.[20]

Another release neatly combined a summary of Shaw's wartime experiences with his present situation and intentions.

> A long hitch in the Navy did Shaw a lot of good. He lived with the other GI's and had little time for his own thoughts and problems. Instead of worrying about the world situation or the lack of new ideas in music, Artie spent his time ducking the bombs that fell from Japanese planes. In the South Pacific Shaw underwent many attacks, often during a performance. He then saw how much music meant to the men in combat. It made Artie realize that there were many things that could be done in music. He is now making full use of that experience.[21]

GAC publicity flyers also claimed (improbably) that a re-formed if not repentant Shaw was preparing to meet—and sat-isfy—popular tastes.

> Artie has taken the public into consideration first and is point-ing every tune at the audiences he'll face. It's quite a change for the high-riding youth who played only what he wanted to during the late thirties when his band was on top. He's still the biggest figure in the music business, but Shaw has ma-

tured after a Navy hitch. From now on it's John Q. Public come [sic] first and foremost in the selection of songs.[22]

Such public relations statements suggested that a chastened and more circumspect Artie Shaw had returned from the Pacific. It remained to be seen whether he would, in fact, adapt to the conditions at home as the war drew to a close. As he quickly discovered, one problem—that of persistent white racism—continued to plague African-Americans.

Trumpeter Roy Eldridge's short tenure with Shaw's first postwar band was marred by several incidents of racial prejudice and discrimination. On one occasion, Eldridge was refused admission to a venue where the Shaw band was appearing—even though his own name was on the marquee outside. Finally allowed entrance, he played the first set with "tears rolling down my cheeks." After the performance, he went to his dressing room, still crying, and recalled that "Artie came in and he was real great. He made the guy apologise that wouldn't let me in, and got him fired." Ava Gardner recounts a similar, if not the same, episode in 1944 when she was with the Shaw band at an engagement in San Diego, and Eldridge failed to appear on the stand.

Artie was furious, so much that he was still steaming when we went out the stage door after the first set to enjoy a cigarette. And there was Roy Eldridge, sitting in the gutter, holding his trumpet and crying, the tears pouring down his cheeks. He hadn't been allowed in the building. He'd been told: "A nigger playing in a white man's band? Don't give us that crap. Get out of here, nigger, if you know what's good for you." Artie was often testy. This time he was not testy, he was volcanic with anger. The result: Roy Eldridge was allowed into the building. At that next set, Roy Eldridge blew his horn until the notes shimmered off the rooftops. He played a tune called *Little Jazz*. In those days, when the kids really liked a number, they stopped dancing and clustered around the bandstand. This time they hemmed in to listen to Roy's fantastic playing. I'll never forget that occasion. Roy stood there blowing his heart out, tears streaming down his face. It was heartbreaking. I wept with him.[23]

Shaw, always a liberal on racial matters, understood and sympathized with Eldridge's situation.

It was very tough for him in my band, just as it had been for Billie Holiday when she was with me in the thirties. When I hired Roy, I told him that he would be treated like everyone else in the band, and that he would be paid very well, because he was the best. I told him that I could handle racial matters when we were on the stand, but there was very little I could do when we were off. Droves of people would ask him for his autograph at the end of the night, but later, on the bus, he wouldn't be able to get off and buy a hamburger with the guys in the band. He thought he was travelling through a hostile land, and he was right. Things came to a head at the San Francisco Auditorium when he arrived late and they wouldn't let him in the main entrance. He was a bitch of a player, and everybody in the band loved him.[24]

For reasons that are unclear, Shaw again disbanded in 1945, but at the end of the year signed with the Musicraft label. On November 14, he recorded three excellent instrumentals: *The Glider*, *The Hornet*, and *Let's Walk*. He also made some sides for

Musicraft with the young jazz vocalist—and Shaw enthusiast—
Mel Tormé, who writes:

> I had been in awe of Shaw for years. Back at Hyde Park High
> [in Chicago], the controversy had raged daily: who is the better
> clarinetist, Goodman or Shaw? I was firmly entrenched in the
> Shavian camp. The Shaw 1939 band was my favourite of that
> era. If I felt like showing off in front of my schoolmates, I
> could rattle off the names of every single member of that
> band.[25]

There is substantial jazz content on such numbers as *What Is
This Thing Called Love?* and *I Got the Sun in the Morning*, and
Tormé credits Shaw for his advice on nuances of inflection on
this last song.

In 1947, Shaw gave up playing jazz for a year, concentrated
on classical music, and was featured with the WOR studios
string quartet in broadcasts of Mozart's *Clarinet Quintet in A
Major* and Russian composer Alexander Krein's *Hebrew Sketches*
(see chapter 7). Listening to these recordings as they were being
prepared for *Book-of-the-Month Club* release in 1984, Shaw provided a commentary on the context of his performances.

> I showed up at the WOR studios one Sunday and talked the
> piece [Mozart's *Clarinet Quintet*] over for a few minutes with
> the string players. They were the staff quartet at the station.
> They had been playing there for some time, and I appeared as
> a guest soloist. We went on the air that Sunday morning and
> played the piece through without rehearsing one note. There
> are some imperfections—a few rubatos, for example. But it's
> OK, I don't mind it being out there.[26]

He also recorded specially commissioned works by composer Alan Schulman—*Mood in Question* and *Rendezvous for Clarinet and Strings*—and in 1948 appeared at Carnegie Hall as guest soloist with Leon Barzin conducting the National Youth Symphony in a performance of Nicolai Berezowsky's *Concerto for Clarinet and Orchestra in B-Flat,* op. 28. Still in a classical vein, Shaw also recorded eight short pieces by Ravel, Debussy, Kabalevsky, and Shostakovitch, adapted for clarinet and symphony orchestra by the arranger Hershey Kay, and conducted by Walter Hendl. Gunther Schuller, who has listened carefully to these (rare) recordings, believes that they reveal another side of Shaw's talent, "his classical playing—that he had previously only touched lightly, easily demonstrating that he could hold his own with any clarinetist in the world, classical or otherwise, including his nemesis, Benny Goodman."[27]

Shaw's increasing preoccupation with classical music was made dramatically apparent to the jazz fraternity when in May 1949 he appeared as the opening attraction (and for a one-week appearance) at Bop City, a new jazz venue at Broadway and West 49th Street in New York City—with a forty-piece "symphony" orchestra. Leonard Feather, who was master of ceremonies on the opening night, reported:

> At 9:30 p.m., Artie's group of strings, woodwinds et al., marched on to the specially enlarged stage. Then Artie himself, looking amazingly young for his 38 years, entered, turned his back on the audience and gave the downbeat. His clarinet was nowhere to be seen. His program comprised music by Koio, Kabalevsky, Debussy, Milhaud, Prokoviev, Finzi, and other pieces.

Poorly received by the patrons with "flurries of sarcastic clapping," Shaw's program at Bop City astonished and outraged the critics. *Metronome* commented that Shaw's "well-staffed organization" was billed as the "big attraction" but it proved to be an "under-rehearsed orchestra, which ran sometimes nervously, sometimes confidently, through a program both light and heavy, all twentieth-century in vintage. Ella [Fitzgerald] really took over after his departure." Shaw did play clarinet during his one-week appearance at Bop City, but neither his playing nor his conducting impressed *Down Beat* critic Mike Levin, who asserted scathingly:

> Never before has such miserable conducting been seen or heard anywhere in the music business. Shaw's concept of leading consists of raising and lowering his arms in what he thinks is approximate conjunction with the beat. Dynamics, shadings, tempo, or any coloration whatsoever are things completely outside his ken or capability. Mr. Shaw is a pretentious young [sic] man who evidently feels his capabilities are completed unlimited, his horizons unbounded. The only things unbounded about him are his ego and his musical ignorance.

Shaw's clarinet playing was described and dismissed as "sterile and stiff" with "a tone of the familiar fire-siren quality" and "clodden heaviness" in which "clinkers were prominent," together with "faulty intonation" in what was, overall, a "second-rate hack performance."[28]

Shaw gave a typically idiosyncratic—and in some respects equally curious—performance of another kind when he appeared later in the year as a subject for Leonard Feather's "Blindfold Test" in *Metronome*.[29] As Feather subsequently related:

I wasn't sure whether we were embarking on a blindfold test, a general interview or a social occasion with no journalistic objectives. It turned out to be a weird combination of all three, and after sorting out in my dazed mind some of the 25,000 words or more that must have been exchanged during the dialogue, I decided [that] a resume of some of the more tangible statements would be worth reporting.

One of these "more tangible statements" concerned saxophonist Boyd Raeburn's recording of *Boyd Meets Stravinsky*, featuring pianist Dodo Marmarosa. Shaw summarily dismissed the performance as "very exhibitionist," and simply an attempt "to show they can play very fast. I don't know where the musical value comes in."[30] Woody Herman's seminal 1946 recording of the four-movement *Summer Sequence*, composed and arranged by Ralph Burns, and featuring trombonist Bill Harris and, most notably, tenor saxophonist Stan Getz, received qualified Shavian approval—for its *arrangement*: "I half enjoy this and half say to myself why doesn't he [Burns] do something with his talents."

After listening to the Dizzy Gillespie orchestra's 1948 recording of *Lover Come Back to Me*—a tour de force for Gillespie's alternately tender and explosive trumpet playing—Shaw asked rhetorically: "What do other people think of these things? Do people buy this? Is music going along these lines? What is the excuse for butchering something?" He then offered his own very decided views on the piece. It was "a negation of the classic definition of music—melody, rhythm and harmony." As for Gillespie's trumpet playing, Shaw asserted that "I'm not interested in him. So he can play high F! Good—bad—by what standards? I'm afraid we're talking in a vacuum."

Gillespie was also present on another recording played by Feather—the 1949 "Metronome All Stars" poll-winners' fluently joyous version of *Victory Ball*. Other "modernists" present on this studio session included Miles Davis and Fats Navarro (trumpets), J. J. Johnson (trombone), Buddy DeFranco (clarinet), Charlie Parker (alto saxophone), Lennie Tristano (piano), and Shelly Manne (drums). Shaw refused to listen to the entire take, commenting brusquely that "it's really no use our going on with this. There just isn't any point of contact. All I can say is, if this is the quintessence of what jazz is doing, I don't want to go back into it."

Asked by Feather for his reactions to bop, Shaw (who was shortly to form his short-lived but most "progressive" orchestra) replied—more reasonably—that he rejected the false swing/bop dichotomy, since he didn't approve of "terms that imply that one thing has stopped and something else has taken over. I'm against the cultist's idea that the old jazz is no good." Pressed to explain what he had been trying to do during his recent engagement at Bop City, Shaw replied that he had wanted "to find out the reaction of a typical American audience to some music that was not the usual fare they're handed," but conceded that "the first night was a mess." Questioned about his "ultimate objectives in music," Shaw immediately saddled and rode his now-familiar hobby horse.

> I'm not interested in keeping a band together—running a band means keeping payrolls and so forth, and that's business. I'm not interested in business. I might get an orchestra together just for once in a while, combining the idea I had at Bop City with another, smaller group playing popular music.[31]

Shaw's 1949 strictures against "bop" and Dizzy Gillespie—
one of its prime exemplars—contrast with Benny Goodman's responses in a Blindfold Test of December 1948, when Feather
played him some recordings by Fats Navarro and Tadd Dameron—both of whom were immediately recognized by Goodman—who also praised Dizzy Gillespie's (unfortunately titled)
Shaw 'Nuff as "a very good record." Neither Shaw nor Goodman
were particularly drawn to the innovations of bop, but the latter's
remarks suggest that he was more in sympathy with this developing form of "modern jazz."[32]

Shaw's statements in 1949 recall Philip Larkin's celebrated
diatribe (twenty years later) against "modernism" in the arts
whether "perpetrated" by "Parker, Pound, or Picasso."[33] But
whereas Larkin, to the end of his life, professed a (not entirely
convincing) abhorrence of "modern jazz," Shaw came to express
an apparently genuine enthusiasm for the bop revolutionaries he
had earlier slighted and dismissed. In the commentary, already
mentioned, which accompanied the release of his 1954 Gramercy Five and earlier recordings, Shaw relates:

> It's pretty hard to continue in a craft and not recognize what's
> going on around you. Once Charlie [Parker] and Dizzy [Gilles-
> pie] and some of the others like Thelonious Monk came along
> and changed the entire face of jazz—actually, they were the
> first wholly new influence since Louis Armstrong—the music
> couldn't possibly have remained the same. They had been lis-
> tening to the same music I listened to all my life, so I never
> was uncomfortable with the "new" chord structures they were
> playing. After Dizzy and Charlie came along I was, for the first
> time in my life as a player, able to stretch out and do what I

had always wanted to do but what audiences wouldn't hold
still for when I was at my zenith. At that time I had to stay
within the frame of what mass audiences understood. So it
was a great relief when the boppers arrived. I was quite comfortable with those guys.[34]

This more considered comment suggests that perhaps Shaw had
become wiser *after* rather than *during* the heady days of the bop
revolution. It's also distinctly possible that during the earlier conversation with Feather, the adversarial Shaw was being deliber-
ately polemical in his denigration of bop.

Following a brief visit to Britain—where, owing to Ministry
of Labour restrictions, he was unable to perform with British musicians—Shaw returned to Hollywood and in August 1945 began
to assemble a new orchestra. Barry Ulanov, in a *Metronome* article the following month, reported that Shaw had said that he was
"not going to lead any jazz revolutions." Instead, he would be
playing music which the public "seems to want from me, music
that's been summed up as '*Frenesi-Begin the Beguine-Stardust*,'"
and for the remainder of the time, "whatever I want to play." As
for *style*, Shaw asserted, "I'll try anything."[35]

One of the things that Shaw now seemed willing to "try"
were arrangements for his new band by such accredited and established "modernists" as Gerry Mulligan, Mary Lou Williams,
Eddie Sauter, and Tadd Dameron—although only the writing of
Dameron appears to have been recorded. Shaw's new orchestra—which included at various times such ex-Woody Herman
alumni as tenor saxophonists Al Cohn, Zoot Sims, Herbie Stew-
ard, and Don Lanphere—with pianist Dodo Marmarosa and guitarist Jimmy Raney, toured in New England, Canada, and the

Mid-West over a two-month period. But when audiences failed to respond to Shaw's new "progressive" sounds, he adopted another tactic. "I had a bandboy named Tommy Thompson," he recalled, "and I told him, 'You're the arranger now. Get the latest copy of *Variety*, pick out the ten top tunes, and buy stock arrangements of them all. That will be the nucleus of our library.'" At whatever personal cost, Shaw also acted the part of a musical clown. "I did all the things I'd shied off from all my life. I laughed, I ogled, I waggled my head, I laid my clarinet over my shoulder and marched, and some S. O. B. in Brooklyn had the gall to tell me: "Artie, this is the best outfit we've had here since Blue Barron.'"[36]

Studio recordings of the Shaw 1949–1950 orchestra (chapter 7) reveal it to have been capable of producing swinging performances of such updated items in the Shavian lexicon as *Begin the Beguine*, *Softly As in a Morning Sunrise*, and *Stardust*, along with more innovative originals like *Krazy Kat*, *Orinoco*, *Innuendo*, and *Fred's Delight*—the last arranged by Tadd Dameron. Shaw's playing on all these (and other) titles is quite superb—lyrical, poised, crystal clear, and, on some numbers, decidedly boppish.

But Shaw—perhaps because of his mortification over the Blue Barron "compliment"—was again losing interest in the musical scene. In March 1950, he took a band—this time playing stock arrangements—into Bop City. Critical responses were, at best, lukewarm. George T. Simon reported that although Shaw had "played fine technical clarinet, sounding most inspired with his smaller group, it was a sorry exhibition from a man who has apparently given up."[37] That Shaw had again—at least temporarily—"given up" the life of a peripatetic band leader was shortly illustrated by his conspicuous absence from the music scene for the next two years.

NOTES

1. *Swing Changes*, 143. Yet as Lewis Erenberg contends, World War II both "highlighted and then exhausted swing as it brought the central tensions of the 1930s to a head. As swing became enmeshed in national purpose, it became more bureaucratic and sentimental. Although Glenn Miller supported [cultural] pluralism, his orchestra was a whitened and corporate version." *Swinging the Dream*, 251.

2. *Ibid.* 9.

3. *Ibid.* 148.

4. See especially Mike Zwerin, *La Tristesse de Saint Louis: Swing Under the Nazis* (London: Quartet Books, 1985), Michael H. Kater, *Different Drummers: Jazz in the Culture of Nazi Germany* (New York: Oxford University Press, 1992), and Ralph Willett, "Hot Swing and the Dissolute Life: Youth, Style and Popular Music in Europe 1939–49," *Popular Music*, Volume 8, No. 2 (1989), 157–63.

5. "Middle Aged Man Without a Horn," 65.

6. Blandford, *Artie Shaw*, 128–9. Whitney Balliett, *American Musicians: 56 Portraits in Jazz* (New York and Oxford: Oxford University Press, 1986),123–4.

7. *My Life in Jazz*, 135.

8. "Middle-Aged Man Without a Horn," 67. Frequently patronized by his superiors, Shaw was disgusted when an officer asked, "Can I shake the hand of the hand that held Lana Turner's tit?" Chris Way, *The Big Bands Go to War* (Edinburgh and London: Mainstream Publishing, 1991), 266.

9. Whitney Balliett, *Barney, Bradley, And Max*. 85.

10. "Middle-Aged Man Without a Horn," 68.

11. *My Life in Jazz*, 143.

12. *The Trouble With Cinderella*, 373. *The Big Bands Go to War*, 266. Not all American troops welcomed press reports of Shaw's military

exploits. "Servicemen in the South Pacific wrote angrily to protest effusive coverage of Artie Shaw's heroic tour that ignored the deprivation experienced by GIs in the trenches." *Swing Changes*, 149–50.

13. *The Big Bands Go to War*, 268.

14. During a 1992 interview Shaw offered another reflection on the war years. "In a way, the war saved my life, because it ended that period of success. By the time I was discharged, I was a wreck and was suffering what we now refer to as post-traumatic stress. I didn't have a clue who I was, so I left the marriage [to Betty Kern] and got into analysis. The Navy had shaken me up pretty good, not to mention the fact that I was confused enough when I enlisted." Kristine McKenna, "Artie Shaw Tells It Like It Is," *LA Weekly*, November 12–18, 1999.

15. Blandford, *Artie Shaw*, 135–6.

16. Whitney Balliett, *New York Notes: A Journal of Jazz, 1972–1975* (Boston: Houghton Mifflin Company, 1976), 106–7.

17. *Little Jazz*, composed by Eldridge and Buster Harding, who also wrote the arrangement, is the only recording of the period on which Shaw does not solo—a mark of his respect for Eldridge.

18. *The Swing Era*, 711.

19. Blandford, *Artie Shaw*. 141.

20. "Nothing Bothers Artie Shaw After Playing for Uncle Sam," Press Information Department. General Artists Corporation, New York City. Artie Shaw File. Institute of Jazz Studies, Rutgers University.

21. "Artie Shaw's Return to Music Welcomed," *Ibid*.

22. "New Artie Shaw Band Called Greatest," *Ibid*. Another GAC release claimed that: "The formula for the success of Artie Shaw is largely based on his musical integrity. Artie Shaw's is a remarkably alert and provocative mind. He is a voracious reader, a stimulating thinker, a seeker after knowledge. When you combine these things with his very great talent as a musician, you have the size and shape of a very large creative force." "Shaw Follows Simple Formula—Music Must Sound Good to Him!" *Ibid*.

23. Nat Shapiro and Nat Hentoff, eds. *Hear Me Talkin' to Ya: The Story of Jazz by the Men Who Made It* (New York: Rinehart, 1955), 320–21; *Ava: My Story* (New York: Bantam Books, 1992). 110–11.

24. Whitney Balliett, "A Hostile Land," *Goodbyes and Other Messages: A Journal of Jazz, 1981–1990* (New York and Oxford: Oxford University Press, 1991), 253; "Little Jazz," *American Musicians: 56 Portraits in Jazz,* 173.

25. Mel Tormé, *It Wasn't All Velvet: An Autobiography* (London: Robson Books, 1989), 88–9. Tormé adds that "Artie is someone with whom working has always been a treat and often instructive. I always regretted his having forsaken the clarinet at a far-too-early retirement from the music business." *Ibid.* 266.

26. Liner notes to "Artie Shaw: A Legacy," (Camp Hill, Pennsylvania: 1984). 13.

27. *The Swing Era,* 713. In an acerbic footnote, Schuller—apparently unaware of Shaw's WOR broadcasts—remarks: "How it must have rankled Shaw to see Goodman engaged by the major symphony orchestras and leading string quartets to perform the works of Mozart, Weber, Debussy, Bartok, Milhaud, Copland! Shaw was obliged to hire his own free-lance orchestra for the 1949 Columbia recordings." More pertinently, Schuller also suggests that given Shaw's admiration for classical composers and penchant for semi-symphonic aggregations, it is perhaps surprising that he was not commissioned to perform Stravinsky's *Ebony Concerto,* written for and performed by Woody Herman. Schuller hazards the guess that perhaps Stravinsky, with his decided jazz sympathies, "preferred the un-bridled string-less excitement of *Caldonia* to the more sedate musical essays of Paul Jordan (or the pretensions of *Concerto for Clarinet*)." *Ibid.* 706.

28. Blandford, *Artie Shaw.* 147–8.

29. Feather instituted the "Blindfold Test" in *Metronome* in 1946, transferring the feature to *Down Beat* in 1951. Jazz musicians were asked to identify—and rate on a five-star scale—the records they heard. As Feather explains: "The objective of the blindfold test is honest subjective reaction. The blindfoldee is always reminded that commercial values are secondary, and that the guessing of an artist's identity is of less consequence that the listener's evaluation on a purely aesthetic level." Feather, "The Jazzman as Critic: The Blindfold Test," *The Encyclopedia of Jazz* (New York: Bonanza Books, 1960), 474.

30. Schuller points out that the Raeburn orchestra's version of *Boyd Meets Stravinsky* echoed the introduction to the African-American bandleader Don Redman's famous 1931 recording of *Chant of the Weed*.

31. Blandford, *Artie Shaw*. 149–52 *passim*.

32. Firestone, *Swing, Swing, Swing*, 348.

33. Philip Larkin, Introduction to *All What Jazz: A Record Diary* (London: Faber and Faber, 1970), 17. Larkin adds mischievously that he cites "these pleasantly alliterative names to represent not only their rightful owners but every practitioner who might be said to have succeeded them." *Ibid.* In a Footnote to the Second Edition of *All What Jazz*, he declares unrepentantly: "If Charlie Parker seems a less filthy racket today (1984) than he did in 1950 it is only because much filthier rackets succeeded him."

34. "Artie Shaw: A Legacy" 10.

35. Blandford, *Artie Shaw*.153–4.

36. "Middle-Aged Man Without a Horn," 93. Blue Barron, the leader of a "Mickey-Mouse" dance orchestra, specialized in "comedy" routines and assorted musical japes that did not have even the most tenuous relationship with big-band swing. George T. Simon described the band's style in a 1938 *Metronome* review as: "obnoxious over-phrasing, saxes with whining vibratos, trumpets that growl and rat-a-tat and slur into harsh, irritating mutes, a trombone that glisses over all creation, all sorts of over-slurring, an electric guitar, a rhythm section that puts most of its emphasis upon a tuba burping on the first and third beat, attempted glee club effects, and all similar, musical tricks that associate corn with commercialism and commercialism with corn." *The Big Bands*, 491. Barron, who once delivered the considered opinion that "Swing is nothing but orchestrated sex, a phallic symbol set to sound, [and] music that cannot shake off its origins in the lowest sporting spots of the Deep South," may not have been too offended by Simon's verdict. Firestone, *Swing, Swing, Swing*, 242.

37. Blandford, 157–58.

Artie Shaw (*Albie Snow*): the writer at work

Cinderella and Other Stories

You try different things—Picasso went through five different phases.

Artie Shaw

Artie Shaw [was] a meshuggener (crazy man) if there ever was one. I roomed with him once. He's been married so many times that you might think he was a swinger—a real gone guy with the broads. But what do you think he did at night? He kept me up—believe it or not—with his typing. He was writing some stories.

Manny Klein

After his "retirement" from the music business in 1950, Shaw bought a cattle farm—"Picardy Farm"—in Pine Plains, Dutchess County, New York. With characteristic thoroughness and application, he studied agricultural reports and attended livestock auctions as far afield as Wisconsin. In retrospect, he remembers this as being "probably the happiest and most self-fulfilling period of my life."[1] From December 1950 until February 1952, he also worked on his autobiography, *The*

Trouble With Cinderella, subtitled *An Outline of Identity*. An essential item in the Shaw oeuvre, it is by turns informative and opaque, entertaining and irritating, concise and convoluted, rewarding and repetitious, as much a cliché-ridden account of Shaw's "philosophy" of life as of his musical career. Despite his assertion that "My essential idea was to tell what I had seen, done, learned, felt etc., while living the life of a white jazz musician in the late twenties and early thirties," there is surprisingly little of substance concerning Shaw's various orchestras. Again, apart from the description of pianist Willie "The Lion" Smith in Harlem, there are only fleeting references to the major jazz musicians Shaw encountered or employed. At its (considerable) worst, Shaw's prose is quite appalling:

> When it comes to final values, I add to the punctuation of the world a tiny question mark. In the vast enigma of the entire universe, I flaunt the childish riddle of myself and my own trifling self-preoccupations. My life is just one more ridiculous toy in the littered cupboard of the spinning galaxies that wheel unendingly through an infinity of time and space.[2]

This overblown and embarrassing passage appears in the concluding chapter, which is prefaced by a quotation from William Butler Yeats: "And I would find myself and not an image." Such verbal excesses call into question Shaw's literary gifts and also, more seriously, the editorial practices of his publishers. Such verbal excesses are the more remarkable, given Shaw's concern to stress his friendships with such notable stylists as William Saroyan, Robert Benchley, Nathaniel West, Dorothy Parker, S. J. Perelman, John O'Hara, John Steinbeck, and Sinclair Lewis.

Their names appear in a text heavily larded with maxims from such luminaries as Lewis Carroll, Kierkegaard, Bernard Shaw, Henri Bergson, Rousseau, Seneca, Voltaire, Ibsen, Samuel Johnson, Walt Whitman, and Shakespeare. Given the triteness and vulgarity of much of Shaw's autobiographical prose, these literary/ philosophical references suggest a flourishing of intellectual credentials and the aggressive self-consciousness of an autodidact.

But *The Trouble With Cinderella* does contain one superlatively written and instructive piece. Prefaced by a line from Virgil—"This is the task, this the labour"—chapter 41 recreates the sights, sounds, and tensions of a swing-band rehearsal. It was reprinted in its entirety in the anthology *Eddie Condon's Treasury of Jazz* with the comment that "it gives an excellent picture of what goes on at a big-band rehearsal."[3] The scene is set in a "big dark basement" at around 1:30 a.m., situated directly under "the polished dance floor of the Roseland State Ballroom, a public dance hall in Boston located about a block from Symphony Hall." Amid a cluster of instruments, music racks and straight-backed chairs, "a Negro boy of twenty-one or so" begins to arrange some order out of the chaos. The musicians themselves, of assorted sizes, shapes, and ages, smoke and chatter, and try out tentative scales on trumpets, saxes, and trombones, while a piano, bass, and guitar provide a subdued undertone to the increasingly raucous proceedings. The leader—"a dark-haired boy of twenty-six or so"—suddenly appears and calls for order. He directs the players to "Get out number seventy-eight" and the men rustle through their scores, looking for "letter C." The leader then taps out the tempo with his foot.

There is complete silence now except for the foot-tapping in regular rhythmic intervals—and then, over the tapping and in time with the tapping, he counts off, one number for each of the two pairs of taps—"one," tap, "two," tap—and suddenly the musicians hit it at "letter C" at the point where count "three" should have come if the leader had gone on counting. Only now, instead of disorganized blaring and gurgling and groaning and bellowing and tinkling and thudding and plunking and plinking and booming, there is the sound of instruments fused in an organized, rhythmic pattern, brass blending into a sectional choir, floating over the rhythmic fusion of drums, piano, bass, and guitar and resting lightly on the trombone-and-low-saxophone base. [T]he trumpets break off in abrupt cessation, the saxophone-and-trombone mixed-choir carry on above the rhythm pulse in a low-voiced blend so interwoven that it is hard to tell which is saxophone and which is trombone. The tune is an old one, of early jazz vintage, *Someday Sweetheart* and at a certain point in the music, just before the melody soars to a high note, the leader cuts in with his clarinet, plays a crisp fill-in phrase, and suddenly takes his clarinet out of his mouth, shouting—"O. K.—hold it, that's the spot I mean."[4]

As a piece of well-constructed, descriptive, and evocative prose, this passage partly compensates for the prolixity, crackerbarrel philosophizing and dubious assertions which are sprinkled liberally throughout *The Trouble With Cinderella*. For example, discoursing on the incompatibility of commerce and art, Shaw pontificates that "popular music has little or nothing to do with musical values at all. It"s fundamentally functional—just one more form of 'entertainment'—and the music is only incidental." Dance-band leaders were dominated by "market-place values . . .

to such an extent that musical ones finally cease to exist."[5] Yet Duke Ellington, Count Basie, Benny Goodman, Woody Herman—and Shaw himself, although more erratically than these contemporaries—contrived to produce music of great quality and universal appeal, despite the pressures of the "market-place."

Gunther Schuller, unimpressed by Shaw's fascination with such pieces as *The Chant* with its "awful fake-voodoo-atmosphere" and tom-tom rhythms, observes:

> How he [Shaw] could chastise fellow musicians for being intellectual pygmies, for not knowing and reading Shakespeare, Balzac, and Joyce, or not listening to Beethoven string quartets, and at the same time consistently produce such trashy numbers as *The Chant, Nightmare, Ubangi,* and *Hindustan—* which the gullible public in its need for exotica, of course, loved, and turned into commercial hits for Shaw—is again one of those confounding contradictions in Shaw's personality.[6]

Shaw's first book raised the eyebrows of its reviewers—if it did not always elicit their most lucid or profound responses. The Chicago *Sunday Tribune* announced that "Shaw has written his story with all the emotion at his command. He has fathomed his own personality in a wise, sensitive manner, and remains optimistic in the face of discouraging reality." Roland Sawyer, in the *Christian Science Monitor*, observed: "The book is written frankly and will be vulgar in a few places for some readers. Perhaps this is because Shaw tried to write as completely an honest account of himself as he could. The life of a jazz musician in America, as revealed here in gripping realism, is not a pretty or hopeful one. [This] is a fascinating narrative of a contemporary American, an absorbing account of a man's struggle with himself." Thomas Sugrue, writing in the New York *Herald Tribune*, announced patronizingly: "No illiterate, this fellow Shaw-Arshawsky, and he has done an impressive job of educating himself in the realities of personal existence, both abstract and concrete. His adventure thus far in life is purely American, yet even in the America of today it is unique." The *New Yorker*, in a less purple and more informative notice, suggested:

> [This] story of the metamorphosis of little Arthur Arshawsky, the son of poor Jewish immigrants, into Artie Shaw, the mercurial jazz-band leader and idol of American youth is a fascinating one, and his dissection of the world of hot music—of what makes a fine musician and a fine jazz band—is as good as anything of the sort in print. His soul-searchings are frequently embarrassing, and he has a marked tendency to babble. But when he has a good grip on himself—and, fortunately, that is more often than not—he is an excellent writer.

Jazz critic Ralph J. Gleason, writing for the *San Francisco Chronicle*, found much to admire in Shaw's autobiographical musings, and surmised that "had he seen fit to discuss his various marriages—and he's had about as many wives as jobs—the book might have been sensational." Rex Lardner, in the *New York Times*, commented somewhat ambiguously that in a recent television appearance Shaw had said that "of all the people in the world, he would most rather be George Bernard Shaw. Well, he is not George Bernard Shaw and he is certainly not Carlyle; but in his own field the young man with a clarinet is perhaps as talented as they and has written a book that deserves to be read—if only because he wrote it."[7]

Although he was increasingly drawn to writing, Shaw had not yet entirely abandoned his intermittent career as a professional musician. One edition of a latter-day Gramercy Five, which never recorded, appeared at a New York Scandinavian restaurant, The Iceland, in the winter of 1950–1951. In fact, it was pianist Billy Taylor's quartet, featuring Shaw. Interviewed by Leonard Feather about his Iceland booking, Shaw was decidedly unenthusiastic:

> I don't know why they even bother to put on a show. What's the point? You stand there and say "Now we're going to play this, or next we'd like you to hear that," and there they are, a bunch of middle-aged women, not hearing, not caring or understanding what you're playing; probably wishing you'd get off so they can get on with their meal.

Asked why he was prepared to play for an uninterested audience, Shaw replied:

> I just came down here to pick up a few fast bucks. It's strictly for the loot. You can't make music any more—the band business as we know it is dead. People don't follow bands and know all the soloists the way they did. The people who have been through a war and want to be reminded of the days before it are not dance band fans any more; they are middle-aged people with families. And if they are a little older they develop a nostalgia for the razz-ma-tazz era of the 1920s. That's why Dixieland has come back. It's not the music, it's everything people are reminded of by it.

When Feather asked him "If you're not interested in the music business, what are you interested in?", Shaw replied laconically, "*Cows*. With me right now it's just a matter of how soon I can get back to my farm. I don't want to go out like Joe Louis. I want to realise when I am through, and I don't want to try and fit in where I don't belong."[8]

Musically, temperamentally, and politically, Shaw did not "belong" in the increasingly conformist America of the early 1950s. On February 9, 1950, Joseph McCarthy, an obscure Republican senator from Wisconsin, caused a sensation with a speech delivered in Wheeling (in his home state) in which he reportedly announced:

> While I cannot take time to name all of the men in the State Department who have been named as members of the Communist Party and members of a spy ring, I have here in my hand a list of two hundred and five that were known to the Secretary of State and who nevertheless are still working and shaping the policy of the State Department.[9]

McCarthy's wild—and totally unsubstantiated—assertions on this occasion drew upon and strengthened American fears of domestic subversion, Communist "conspiracies," unorthodox opinions, and "deviant" behavior in the era of the Cold War. Harold H. Velde, a former FBI agent, was a Republican congressman who had campaigned on the slogan "Get the Reds out of Washington and Washington out of the Red." At the end of 1952, he was the chairman-designate of the Committee on Un-American Activities (HUAC), which quickly turned its attention to "subversion" in the Hollywood and New York entertainment worlds. There were elements of farce (as well as of personal tragedy) in the committee's investigations. During its hearings in Los Angeles, it transpired that one "undercover" FBI agent was a sixty-eight-year-old grandmother, while another agency source reported that "Communists" were allegedly distressed by American radio soap operas because they did not portray the role of women in the revolutionary struggle. Film producers, directors, and actors were summoned before the committee, and some "informed" on their friends and colleagues—who were subsequently blacklisted—with their careers and reputations ruined.[10]

In 1953, Shaw was asked to appear before HUAC. An item in the Los Angeles Times reported: "House Communist hunters disclosed today that much-married band leader Artie Shaw will be the lead-off witness in New York on Monday at hearings on Red activities in the metropolitan area." In his testimony before the Committee, Shaw—with tears welling in his eyes—announced that he was not sure if he had ever been a Party member, but had probably been "a dupe." He "confessed" that "I was certainly a bad Communist. It was never my intention to be one, and to the best of my knowledge I have never been one, although these people may have assumed I was, as I could probably assume some of those people were." He also claimed that he'd had refused to join the Communist Party after attending four "cloak and dagger" meetings in 1946, because he favored freedom of speech, and was now "relieved" to be able to clarify what he termed three years of "haze and rumours" about his past. An abject Shaw fervently promised that he would not again sign anything of a possibly incriminating nature "unless I had the advice of seven lawyers and the granting of permission or clearance by this Committee."[11]

In the course of his forty-five page testimony (during which he admitted joining such "subversive" organizations as the Hollywood Independent Citizens Committee of the Arts, Science, and

Professions, the American Peace Mobilization and several other groups) and in one of several emotional outbursts before the Committee—during which he used his hands to cover his eyes— Shaw announced:

> I would just like to say one thing. This is no prepared statement, or anything. It may sound garbled, but I have, I think, personally, a very large stake in this country, and I want to do anything I can, as I always have, to defend American institutions and American folkways. This country has been very kind to me. I started out as a minority member of a poor family, and I have come a long way for a guy like me; and I have found on the road [that] I am met with a lot of love and a lot of affection, and when I was serving in the service that same thing happened. I never had any intention of doing anything detrimental or disloyal to the interests of this country.

Shaw's fervent testimony, denying his Communist links or sympathies—won Chairman Velde's approval. At the end of the proceedings, he shook Shaw's hand and congratulated him, and before he was excused as a witness, the entire Committee thanked an overwrought Shaw for his co-operation.[12]

A newspaper photograph taken at the time shows Shaw apparently tearful and full of remorse after the hearings. One headline proclaimed: "Band Leader Artie Shaw Had Tears In His Eyes," with the sub-text: "Told House probers he had been dupe of Communists." Shaw—who frequently contrived to run with the hare and the hounds—has always vehemently denied this story, maintaining that the blinding lights of press photographers in fact produced his apparent tears of remorse. An Associated

Press report carried the heading: "Artie Shaw Asserts He Never Was Red, As Far As He Knows."

Shaw has since declared (unconvincingly) that he had only "total contempt" for the HUAC proceedings and was "shocked by some of the questions"—including his alleged support for the World Peace Congress. He asserts that "I tried to walk a narrow line between not informing on anybody and not saying I plead the Fifth Amendment." In 1962, he told *New Yorker* writer Robert Lewis Taylor: "I was in favour of a 'World Peace Congress' [and] I put my name to any group identified with words I was interested in, like *democracy* and *peace*, but I never got close to Communism. Out of curiosity, I attended a couple of Communist meetings under the name of Witherspoon, but I asked so many impertinent questions that they told me: 'Witherspoon, you aren't Communist material.'" In the Introduction to the second edition of *The Trouble With Cinderella*, Shaw is less than candid (or accurate) about either his involvement with or the consequences of his appearance before HUAC.

> Anybody out there still remember the so-called McCarthy Era? Joe McCarthy, that is. Of course—good old Joe, the sterling Super-American, the man who knew exactly what *Un-American* meant because he knew exactly what America meant and was by God going to see to it that America remained American. It's almost impossible, now, to believe it all really happened. Well, O. K. I lived through that particular little firestorm. As an invited guest of the House Un-American Activities Committee. The whole shot. And watched the grey pall fall over my entire life as a direct result of having been branded a 'controversial figure'—meaning, in simpler and more direct terms, an Untouchable."

Shaw's appearance and testimony before HUAC was not his finest hour. Lewis Erenberg—who has studied the entire transcript—relates that Shaw informed the committee that after his demobilization in 1945

> [He] was angry at domestic reactionaries and black marketeers and set out to fight for a Fair Employment Practices Committee and other leftist causes as part of his conception of American war ideals. He confessed to being "duped" and pledged to "defend American institutions and American folkways" and never to sign any petitions or protest letters again. He also swallowed his anger at the anti-Semitism that had scarred his personality and the racism that had marred his attempts to integrate. Instead, he expressed his gratitude for what the nation had done for him, "a member of a minority." Humiliated by having to repudiate his former beliefs, Shaw exiled himself to Spain.[13]

In addition to his traumatic appearance (and questionable performance) before the Velde committee, Shaw also faced a $80,000 federal back-tax claim. To raise the required amount, he had to sell his farm and go on tour with a hastily assembled band. Almost certainly, he found the experience both demoralizing and debilitating, but tried to disguise such feelings in a *Metronome* article (September 1953).

> Being a soloist has its limitations. I know that after having played *Begin the Beguine* I don't know how many thousands of times. I've long passed the stage where I can find something new to play. There just aren't that many combinations of notes to fit the chords. But I find that if I don't think of the other

times that I've played it before, I get much more of a kick out of it. Each version is a new one to me. I may play it in Dallas in 1953 and that's the Dallas 1953 version. Then I may play it in Hartford a month later and that becomes the Hartford 1953 version. I can really make believe and convince myself that this is the first time that I'm playing this, and it shows both in my playing and also in my attitude toward my audiences. I can sense that they feel I'm pretty happy in what I'm doing [and] believe me, I'm having much more of a ball playing with my band even though we repeat an awful lot of numbers, than I've had in years.

On his recently completed tour, audiences had demanded such staples of the Shavian repertoire as *Begin the Beguine, Back Bay Shuffle*, and *Traffic Jam*, and Shaw reflected:

It didn't surprise me; I'd expected it. Four years ago I started off with a great band with a full book of modern things by Johnny Mandel and Tad Dameron and Eddie Sauter and really fine arrangers like that. But by the time we had finished the tour in New York, I wanted to break up the band because hardly anyone wanted to hear those great things we were playing. They wanted the standards I mentioned and the popular tunes of that era. This time, before we started out, I told the booker in Texas, where we played most of our dates, that I wanted to bring down a good band, like the one I started out with last time. I figured, or hoped, that things had improved since then, because everyone seemed to be talking about bands and good music coming back. He told me that if I did he wouldn't guarantee me a successful trip, because what the promoters wanted was my old recorded stuff, so I dug out the 1937 book and we did have a terribly successful trip.

A more tolerant Shaw, it appeared, now enjoyed—or was prepared to accept—catering to the expectations of his audiences, and with unconscious irony (given his earlier comments on the "humiliating compromises" which he had been forced to make) lamented the fact that his sidemen had not been so adaptable.

> The guys did what they had to do well enough. It was a job for them and that was that. It's too bad, though, that they couldn't have had as good a time as I did. I know I'm older and more mature than they are, and maybe I've done a bit more reading and studying, but I wish that at least some of them could have adopted that attitude I've been talking about. I think they would have felt much more satisfied both with their music and with themselves. And it's quite possible that both they and the audience would have heard better music, and have had a lot more fun. I know I certainly did.[14]

In September 1953, Shaw went into the Embers Club in New York City with a new Gramercy Five unit—actually a sextet—with Shaw on clarinet, Joe Roland (vibraphone), Hank Jones (piano), Tal Farlow (guitar), Tommy Potter (bass), and Denzil Best (drums). *Metronome* duly reported:

> Artie is magnificently himself; rather immutable but hardly dated. He uses an inverted megaphone into which he occasionally blows to get an effect remarkably like a sub-tone clarinet. Whether in old or new tunes, in or out of the megaphone, he played with delicacy, purity and facility not at all dimmed by the due process of years.

The other members of the group also received favorable mention.

> Joe Roland is playing the best vibes of his career, crisp, deci-
> sive and swinging, yet with a delicacy the style calls for. Hank
> Jones's piano is similarly improved. Tal [Farlow] does thrilling
> things with one or all the strings. Bassist Tommy Potter swings
> as is his wont, and Denzil Best blows the kind of drums for
> which he is famous. Within a framework of cute, sometimes
> clever arrangements, the solos were of consistently high qual-
> ity, making this one of the top musical groups in the country,
> whose essence promises greater things with maturity.[15]

Time magazine reported Shaw's return to the "music business" at the Embers and remarked that, on the first evening, he
"sounded like a musical D[isplaced] P[erson], playing as if he
could not decide between his own swing style and something
considerably more glittery and progressive." But:

> As the early crowd gave way to the late one, the little band
> began to perk up. Vibraphonist Joe Roland bent over his in-
> strument like a chef over a hot stove. Shaw began to interpo-
> late light-hearted musical comments on his own flights—the
> raised eyebrow of a grace note, the shrugging arpeggio, the de-
> layed take, the impudent echo. His glum face relaxed into
> smiles, and the crowd began to hear the new Artie Shaw. With
> his balding head now shaved ascetically, he is far from the dis-
> traught young hero who deserted his bandstand and disap-
> peared into Mexico 14 years ago, and far, he says, from the
> compulsive husband who married and divorced six times.[16]

Variety, the cheerfully vulgar and ungrammatical newspaper
of the show-business fraternity, reported that "this gig is strictly

for listening and he [Shaw] is dishing it out in socko style." The reconstituted Gramercy Five "is belting out the kind of rhythm that hasn't been heard in these parts for some time." Shaw's clarinet playing, although "it might lack some of the free-wheeling spirit of the '30s, now has a maturity that gives it an added listening appeal. [The] Fact that he holds tablers through sets running to about 45 minutes is a tribute to his musicianship." It noted further that "Shaw has his head shaved, several degrees below crew cut, for this stand, but unlike Samson, he has lost none of his power."[17] *Billboard* also lavished praise on Shaw's performances at the Embers.

> The spark of the new Gramercy Five is all Artie Shaw, tho [*sic*] the boys do yeoman work with him. When he is playing clarinet the group has a brightness and sparkle and it swings; when he is not—you're hearing just another good jazz unit. Shaw showed that he can still play a lot of clarinet, and he retains the identifiable tone that helped put him on top of the heap years ago. He isn't playing the same exciting type of clarinet that he once did, but this could be due to the warm, cozy style he is trying to achieve with the new group. There seems to be little question that the new Artie Shaw Gramercy Five could prove to be a strong attraction for class clubs where musical entertainment is the big draw. The group is smooth, and the tunes should please any crowd. It may not thrill the real gone jazz cats looking for musical excitement, but it will draw many others. The Shaw name should still be potent at the box office.[18]

The *New Yorker* reported that Shaw, "who in recent years has only now and then picked up the clarinet that made him Benny

Goodman's closest rival in the mid-thirties." was "playing as well as ever, with the same fine tone and the same easy invention." More remarkably, perhaps, Shaw himself "appeared unruffled by the noisy audience, in contrast to his celebrated touchiness of past years." Yet the group's performances left something to be desired. A rendition of *Frenesi*, with a Latin-American background, had bowled along merrily for the first chorus. "Then the Six noodled around somewhat aimlessly for a few choruses in straight jazz fashion, after which they rode the number out to its finish, in much the same way they had begun." With seasoned and mutually acquainted musicians, the *New Yorker*'s critic concluded, such "leeway" could result in magnificently improvised performances. But Shaw had effortlessly eclipsed his sidemen, playing "beautifully, and always with the composure of a true artist."[19]

That Shaw was well aware of the radical changes which had already taken place in jazz—and his own cautious responses to them—was evident in an article in which he explained the partly didactic/proselytizing purpose underlying his new small group. Most listeners, he suggested (reflecting his experiences at the Embers) did not possess "the musical background to comprehend the complex forms most of our better young musicians are now playing." But, if they were provided with "a simple melodic framework," audiences would appreciate—and respond to—the more complex forms of jazz. Unfortunately, the dominance in popular music of "honkers and wailing vocalists of both sexes" had dulled the sensibilities of the postwar generation, and Shaw doubted if he would "live to see a mass preference for good instrumental jazz over gimmicked vocal arrangements." He had made a related point in *The Trouble With Cinderella*.

> [No] matter how much rehearsal a band gets, no matter how skillfully and carefully the arrangements are tailored to the abilities of the men playing them, there is still nothing that can take the place of appearing night after night in front of audiences. The very tension that results from being aware of an audience is one of the biggest single factors in smoothing out the rough edges and polishing the surface of a band.[20]

The Embers engagement was to be Shaw's final public appearance as a playing leader. Fortunately, this last—and most underrated—Gramercy Five was captured on record (see chapter 7).

For the next five years, Shaw lived in Spain, where he designed and found a contractor to build a magnificent house, set in the hillside of the medieval village of Bagur on the Costa Brava. He spent his time fishing, writing, and making occasional visits to Rome and Paris. It was on one of his trips to Paris that Shaw (now divorced from Kathleen Winsor) met and married (in Gibraltar) the movie actress Evelyn Keyes—who had formerly been the wife of film director John Huston. In Brigitte Berman's documentary, Ms. Keyes speaks fondly of their life together in Spain, of Shaw's "hobbies" of fishing and astronomy (both of which he carried to the point of professionalism), his wide-ranging reading and well-stocked library, and his compulsive tidiness—which included an insistence on the fixing of toilet rolls to unwind from the front and not the back. "Every time I change a toilet roll," she recalled, years after their divorce, "I think of Artie Shaw."

It was in Spain that Shaw returned to his second (if not his first) love of writing, working on the three short stories which would be published in 1955 as *I Love You, I Hate You, Drop Dead! Variations on a Theme*. Surprisingly—given the excesses and longeurs of *The Trouble With Cinderella*—Shaw's first venture into fiction was much better than might have been anticipated. The aptly titled "Grounds for Divorce" examines the breakdown in communication between a magazine editor, Buddy, and his dreadful wife, Marjorie, following her sabotage of an unusual arrangement by which he had agreed to buy back a prized watch, given to him by his father, and appropriated by a mugger.[21] The neat plot and deft handling of dialogue evoke shades of John O'Hara, while in its suspicion of women, the story may offer clues as to why the author himself was divorced so often. "Old Friend" describes and delineates the break-up of a marriage after a virulently anti-Semitic husband discovers that his wife is Jewish, and the narrator's direct addressing of the reader also recalls an O'Hara story, "Pal Joey." "Whodunit," the third "Variation" (which unconsciously anticipates Anthony Shaffer's *Sleuth*) charts the stormy and jealous relationship of a TV producer and the sponsor of his show   the head of a cosmetics company, who is also his wife.

Shaw's first work of fiction received considerable critical acclaim. Terry Southern (author of the classic novel of "soft" pornography, *Candy*) felt that the stories offered "a deeply probing examination of the American marital scene," and judged the writing to be "swift, deft—but never superficial." Frederic Morton believed that Shaw's trilogy "reveals the hypocrisies, pretensions and foibles of men and women. Mr. Shaw gets many of his most highly charged and insightful effects in an apparently incidental, conversational and therefore spontaneous manner." Robert Lewis Taylor, already familiar with Shaw's checkered career, observed:

> The subject matter here discussed is love, marriage and divorce, an area in which Artie Shaw is uniquely, and perhaps painfully, expert. Students of these touchy human relationships will seize on these stories with glee, prizing them as, among other things, valuable precursors of the undoubted Shavian works to come.

In many respects, these highly readable stories offer more revealing insights into Shaw's perceptions of the relations between men and women than the self-serving platitudes offered in *The Trouble With Cinderella*. For example: "when a fellow has been married as often as I have, there's one distinct conclusion that you must arrive at about him—he is seeking some sort of solution to his basic loneliness, trying to solve this problem within the established forms of the culture he happens to be living in."[22]

In 1953, the Shaws moved back to the United States and bought a large house in Lakeville, Connecticut. Here Shaw opened a rifle range, manufactured guns, became an expert competitive marksman, formed a film-producing company (its first release was also its greatest hit—*Seance on a Wet Afternoon*, starring Richard Attenborough and Kim Stanley), appeared on TV and radio shows, and lectured on music at Yale. After separating from Evelyn Keyes (they were later divorced, but remain on good terms) Shaw moved to California in 1973, purchased a house on Outpost Drive in the Hollywood Hills, and taught a seminar in local colleges on the interaction of aesthetics and economics that he called "Three Chords for Beauty, and One to Pay the Rent." He also contributed to the sound track of the motion picture *The Man Who Fell to Earth*—a science-fiction vehicle for rock star David Bowie. In 1978, Shaw moved from Los Angeles to a comfortable house in Newbury Park, in the Conejo Valley, and since then has continued to write, oversee the new Artie Shaw Orchestra, appear on local radio and TV stations, entertain like-minded friends, and regard the rest of humanity with a cynical eye.

The Best of Intentions and Other Stories was published in 1989, although some pieces were written in the 1940s. Shaw's second collection of fiction is, in many ways, superior to his first, and two of the stories have obvious autobiographical content. "Snow White in Harlem, 1930," retails the meeting between the narrator, Al Snow, a young clarinet and saxophone player with a Harlem stride pianist. Wandering around Harlem, "hoping to run across a jam session someplace," Al hears the sound of a piano coming from the basement of an old tenement building at the corner of 134th Street and Lenox Avenue. He is immediately transfixed.

> This cat sounded like some kind of an unlikely combination of Fats Waller and Earl Hines, with a touch of James P. Johnson, Scott Joplin, and Jelly Roll Morton, plus a little Meade Lux Lewis or even Albert Ammons or even Pine Top Smith thrown in for good measure.

Al meets the pianist—"a burly looking coloured guy"—when he emerges onto the sidewalk and discovers that the basement is, in fact, the "Begonia Club" or "Bob's 'n' Sherry's." The pianist introduces himself as "Eddie White"—better known the "The Tiger"—and invites Al into the club where he is acutely conscious of being the only white person present. Invited by his new acquaintance to sit in, Al chooses *I Got Rhythm* and despite his nervousness turns in a creditable performance, after getting used to "The Tiger's" eclectic style—"quite different from anything he had ever heard before" with a "funny choppy-sounding, semi-rag-time-y type of beat"—accompanied by snorts and grunts. Asked by his new patron where he was from, Al tells him that he has recently arrived from Chicago, where he had listened to Louis Armstrong, Earl Hines, Jimmy Noone, Jack Teagarden and Henry "Red" Allen. On reflection, Al decides not to tell "TheT-iger" about his enthusiasm for "people like Debussy and Stravinsky and Bartok." The remainder of the story recounts Al's meeting with a black transvestite singer called "Gloria Swanson" who specialized in obscene and suggestive versions of songs like *Honeysuckle Rose*, and "The Tiger's" assurance that "Bob"—who had bought the club to listen to the kind of jazz that he liked—was certain to invite Al back to play every night.

"A Nice Little Post-War Business" is a first-person narrative of the experiences of a band leader aboard a US Navy ship in the Pacific during World War II. It recounts a surreal and comic conversation between the anonymous narrator and "Sammy"—one of the members of his band—about possible occupations in civilian life. These include breeding giant bullfrogs, opening a fly farm, or raising silver foxes. "Sammy" as he is described in the story is a thinly disguised Max Kaminsky.

Sammy was one of the guys in my outfit. Before the war he had worked in my band for a year or so, and before that I had known him around New York for a number of years. Sammy had a reputation as one of the better jazz trumpet men around town, and always managed to earn his coffee and doughnuts and a few bourbons on the side by working in one or another of those little jazz joints on 52nd Street or the Village, where the Hot Club boys with the crew-cuts used to hang out and discuss Jazz In The Context of Indigenous American Folk Culture. When I joined the Navy and began putting together a service band to take overseas, Sammy joined up too, and we arranged to have him transferred to my outfit.[23]

In "The Fabulous Courtship of Joe Kubak," the eponymous hero, a movie addict and "the owner of a combination delicatessen-lunchroom in Kenosha, Wisconsin" convinces himself that he has married the film star Bette Davis. In this instance, Shaw's appreciation of slang serves wonderfully to place Joe as both a provincial and as a man who thinks he is up-to-the-minute: "Hotsy-totsy"/"oakie-doakie." The story is clever in conception and execution. One knows that this is a (very) tall tale, but goes along with it to see where Shaw will go. It is also "post-modernist" in its readiness to confuse the reader with shifting planes of reality: Joe is fictional, but Bette Davis actually existed.

The remaining stories are less satisfying. "A Stolen Story" is as convoluted as "Joe Kubak," but the narrator, a man who always knows best and despises his friends, is a lot more unpleasant than Shaw seems to realize. "Let George Do It" concerns two friends, Joe and Steve, and their rifle-firing confrontations with pheasants—and themselves—set in what appears to be rural upstate New York. The title story is less satisfying than the original version, *Grounds for Divorce*, contained in *I Love You, I Hate You, Drop Dead!*, which had a strong post-World War II ambience, whereas the update seems to take place in limbo.

Currently, Shaw is working on his magnum opus, a fictionalized account of the life of a jazz musician that will be titled *The Education of Albie Snow*. As he informed a reporter in 1990:

> It deals with the making of a musician, starting in that period when dance music started becoming *jazz*, and when guys who wanted to play jazz in a band had no place to go. White guys, that is. You couldn't play with black bands in those days, or black guys with white bands. That was the state of the world then. So I'm writing something that, as far as I know, I'm uniquely qualified to write. I was *there*.[24]

That Shaw (then in his seventy-fourth year) was also very much *here* insofar as knowing what he wanted from his reformed orchestra was very evident in his responses during a telephone conversation with the late Rod Soar, jazz presenter for Pennine Radio, which was published in 1984. Asked how the orchestra (fronted by clarinetist Dick Johnson) was bedding down, Shaw (echoing the theme of his splendid chapter in *The Trouble With Cinderella*) responded:

> It's very difficult to get a band of this size playing with the precision that it really requires in order to render the kind of music that I am playing properly—you can't do it with rehearsal alone. You can use rehearsal to indicate and finally drill the men to do precisely what you want, but it takes at least a month to three months for it to shape down properly. People have to learn how to breathe together and make their vibratos

match, blend, and mesh in such a way that the saxophone section sounds like one man doing a five note chord.

Queried whether the new band would be playing the old arrangements of Shaw favorites, the reply was interesting—and familiar.

> I determined when I started this band [that] I wasn't going to
> do it as a clone of myself. I didn't want the band to sound like
> it did in the late thirties and early forties. I wanted to retain
> the identity of the band and utilise the same sounds, arrange-
> ments, orchestrations and so on of that band, and play the
> tunes which are identified with my name and my orchestra.
> But I didn't want them played the way they used to be. We are
> playing with a contemporary sensibility, because the musi-
> cians and the type of playing that contemporary musicians are
> capable of is totally different from that of the '38–'39, '40–'42
> period. So what we are doing is playing more or less the same
> notes but the music is quite different, the whole approach is
> different, as is the authority and bite and attack that these
> men provide. I promised myself that I was going to get this
> band to a point where it would sound as though I had played
> right through from the time I broke it up to the present.

Asked if his re-formed orchestra (like its predecessors)
would be presenting "classical swing music," Shaw—always concerned with semantics—expressed his persistent unease with
the word *swing*.

> *Swing* was a publicist's word, when they talk about "swing
> music" that was jazz music, and there were big bands playing
> it and small bands playing it, but jazz must swing and if it
> doesn't swing it isn't jazz. That's why swing is, as far as I'm
> concerned, a verb, not an adjective and not a noun.[25]

Shaw's grammatical distinction goes to the heart of things, and continues to inform the work of the Artie Shaw Orchestra—even if his incomparable clarinet is absent. Recordings of the 1980s and 1990s demonstrate that under the careful guidance of its founding father the band was recreating and recasting the distinctive and joyous sounds of swing. They do not just play *swing* (noun); the whole ensemble *swings* (verb), and does so in a fashion that is as authentic as it is felicitous.

NOTES

1. *The Trouble With Cinderella: With a New Introduction by the Author*, v.

2. *Ibid*. 393. That Shaw's *autobiographical* prose has hardly improved over time can be gauged from his introduction to the 1978 edition of the book: "And so time slogged on. And wrought its many wonders. Not the least of which was the miracle by which an earnest young cat like me (of all people) apotheosized into a fully-fledged show-biz celeb during a wacky decade or more now known as the Swing Era." xii.

3. Eddie Condon and Richard Gehman, eds. *Eddie Condon's Treasury of Jazz* (New York: Dial Press, 1957), 330–39. Condon and Gehman also note that "A musician we know, upon hearing that Artie Shaw had written a kind of autobiography called *The Trouble With Cinderella* responded, 'Why doesn't he call it *The Trouble With Artie?*'" 330.

4. *The Trouble With Cinderella*, 314–20.

5. *Ibid*. 380.

6. *The Swing Era*, 697.

7. *Book Review Digest 1952*, 806. *Pace* Gleason's remark, Shaw deserves credit for refusing to sensationalize his memoirs by including prurient details of his "various marriages." More recently, Gene Lees has generously commended *The Trouble With Cinderella* as "an unspar-

ing and self-searching essay on the life of one troubled man living in a fame-crazed America," and asserts (implausibly) that: "It is an extremely well-written and literate book [which] implicitly expressed a peculiarly American belief that one can do more than one thing well." *Meet Me At Jim & Andy's*, 77.

8. Blandford, *Artie Shaw*, 158–9.

9. Richard H. Rovere, *Senator Joe McCarthy* (London: Methuen, 1960), 101–2.

10. Walter Goodman, *The Committee: The Extraordinary Career of the House Committee on Un-American Activities* (New York: Farrar, Straus and Giroux, 1968).

11. Victor S. Navasky, *Naming Names* (New York: The Viking Press, 1980), 73. Navasky terms Shaw an "uninformed informant."

12. Michael David Whitlatch, *The House Committee on Un-American Activities Entertainment Hearings and their Effects on Performing Arts Careers.* Ph.D. dissertation. (Ohio: Bowling Green State University, 1977), 184–5.

13. "Middle-Aged Man Without a Horn," 68. *Swinging the Dream*, 243.

14. Blandford, *Artie Shaw*, 160–62.

15. "Artie Shaw," *Metronome* (December 1953), 19. Shaw's publicity agent, Virginia Wicks, released an upbeat statement regarding the new Gramercy Five. Marking his "official return to music [Shaw] considers it his most serious venture. He devoted the summer months of '53 to writing for the group and spending three to six hours a day in rehearsal." At its opening night on October 5, 1953 at the Embers "thousands of people were turned away from the doors. Groups milled about on the sidewalk to catch the strains of the Shaw music. A two-week engagement became one of eight weeks, while additional bookings poured in from clubs and theatres throughout the country. The kind of music played by the Gramercy 5? The great Shaw classics, of course. And also jazz for tomorrow, for as ever, Shaw believes in forging ahead!" Artie Shaw File. Institute of Jazz Studies, Rutgers University.

16. "Native's Return," *Time*, October 19, 1953.

17. "Artie Shaw & Gramercy 5, Embers, N. Y.," *Variety*, October 14, 1953.

18. "Shaw Unveils Commercial, Cooler Combo," *Billboard*, October 17, 1953.

19. "Tables For Two: The Pied Piper," *New Yorker*, October 17, 1973.

20. Artie Shaw, "Dixie, Swing, Bop or What?" *See Magazine*, Sept. 1954. Shaw also noted perceptively that: "As one of the few musicians trying to make a musical bridge between the generations, I understand why audiences still cling emotionally to the music of the big swing band. It flourished in the 1938–40 period, the peak of contact between musicians and listeners." *Ibid.* 308.

21. It was to appear in a revised form as the title story in Shaw's second collection of fiction, *The Best of Intentions and Other Stories* (1989).

22. *I Love You, I Hate You, Drop Dead! Variations on a Theme by Artie Shaw* (New York: Fleet Publishing Corporation, 1965). Dust jacket notices. George Plimpton commented more mischievously: "A fine clutch of stories. Emerson once said that genius is a bad husband and an ill provider. How unfortunate for Evelyn Shaw!" *Ibid.* 362.

23. This story also conveys the uncertainties of life aboard US Navy ships in the Pacific during the war. "I can't say how things were in any other war, but in the only one I was ever in it seemed as though you were always aboard some ship bound for some place or other, but nobody ever told you where. As usual the scuttlebutt was running wild all over the ship. One day a rumour would get started that we were on our way to New Caledonia, next day it would be the Aleutians, then one of the messcooks would say he'd overheard the navigation officer telling the gunnery officer about the climate on Espiritu Santo."

24. Tom Nolan, "Still Cranky After All These Years," *Los Angeles*, May 1990. 114. Shaw also informed Nolan: "Fourteen hundred pages so far. I just passed chapter 76. I'd say I'm about seven chapters from the end." *Ibid.*

25. Rod Soar, "The Beguine Begins Again," *Jazz Journal International*, 37 (Dec. 1984).

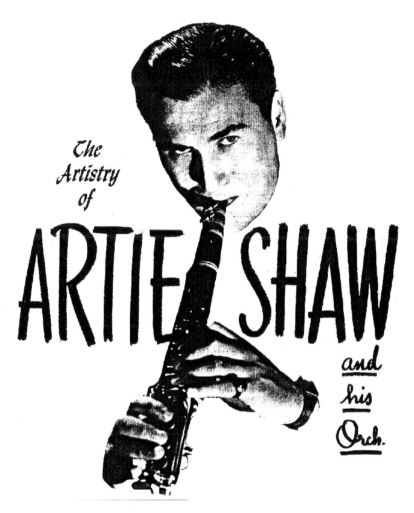

The
Artistry
of

ARTIE SHAW

and
his
Orch.

General Artists Corporation publicity flyer, c. 1934

Concerto for Clarinet:
The Artistry of Shaw

Artie Shaw was probably the greatest natural clarinetist. He had an impossible range. But he suffered from other things. He felt it was beneath his dignity to sign autographs and play for dancers, so he finally just took a walk.

Woody Herman

Artie Shaw was a hell of a clarinet player. My time was always more legato than his, but his sound was more open. It carried a lot farther.

Benny Goodman

In 1985, Tsuyen Hirai, a student of the clarinet, sent tapes of Shaw's *Concerto for Clarinet* (1940) and *Besame Mucho* (1953) to the Japanese solo clarinetist of the Symphonisches Berlin—who had never heard Shaw perform on record or in person. The reply which Hirai received contained the statement: "I've never heard a clarinetist with such enormous technique. If he wanted to play contemporary music, he could play whatever he wanted—perfectly!"[1] Two years earlier, Yoel Levi, conductor of the Cleveland Orchestra, decided to perform Shaw's *Concerto for Clarinet* and obtained a transcribed copy of his solo. When Franklin Cohen, the orchestra's chief clarinetist saw the musical score, he did not anticipate any problems. But when he heard a tape of Shaw's actual performance, Cohen related, "I told Yoel he was crazy," and continued:

> Shaw was unbelievable. He could improvise endlessly, on and on. He was an amazing talent. Shaw's the greatest player I ever heard. It's hard to play the way he plays. It's not an overblown orchestral style. He makes so many incredible shadings.[2]

Jazz critic John McDonough is equally commendatory—and even more specific—about Shaw's clarinet virtuosity. Although he was prepared to "take melodic chances with daring phrases," Shaw was not, McDonough suggests, a musical revolutionary. Rather, his genius resided in a tone "which gave substance and often majesty to his ideas." Shaw's control of tone was most impressive in the upper register, and "he was capable of pulling off sudden leaps into the highest ranges that startled the ear and pierced the senses." Shaw's break on *Non-Stop Flight* (1938) provides a classic example of this enviable ability. In addition, Shaw was a superlative blues player—the acid test for any jazz instrumentalist or vocalist, and McDonough cites the two-part performance of William Grant Still's *The Blues* (1937), where Shaw's "intense vibrato in the highest register can make a listener shiver." This comment would apply equally to Shaw's dazzling solo on *The Blues*—based on *St. Louis Blues* by W. C. Handy, which he performed with the Paul Whiteman Orchestra at Carnegie Hall the following year (see chapter 7).

McDonough also offers a comparative perspective on Shaw's extremely personal style, and suggests that like Sidney Bechet, Shaw's "sound was so much his own that he did not spawn a school of imitators." Again, compared with Benny Goodman, Shaw was an iconoclast who "played little clusters of notes in which the tones were often smeared together, so as to create scoops of sound," while his "swift flights, spanning all registers, were often accented by sudden diminuendos and crescendos that gave his legato a slurred effect." Precisely because his phrases were "seamless," Shaw possessed the technique to create long improvisational lines "stretching out across several bars." Again, *Non Stop Flight* (1938) exemplifies this remarkable skill.

Schuller offers a very similar assessment of Shaw's artistry, suggesting that by 1939 he "had progressed from a proficient imitator of Benny Goodman to a real master of the clarinet, virtually incomparable in the beauty of his tone and unique in the flawless control of the instrument's higher register. Primarily a lyric player, Shaw excelled in his peak years in the long, flowing, seamless soaring line." But Schuller adds pertinently that although Shaw "eventually learned to play with considerable rhythmic verve, swing [as a verb] was not his *forte*. Indeed, it was his weakness in the early years, and an element of his playing which was at best variable, dependent a great deal on the swing capabilities of his rhythm sections."[3]

Among jazz critics, Whitney Balliett has come the closest to evoking a musician's *sound* in words. Philip Larkin observed that he "belongs to the *reportage* school of criticism, in which at least half the writer's talent goes into making you *hear* or *see* the cricket, the boxing, the jazz."[4] Balliett's description of Artie Shaw's artistry illustrates the truth of Larkin's tribute:

> He had an innocent, delicate, impeccably tailored style. His tone was not robust. In the low register, he was soft and convincing, but he lacked the velvet spaces of Goodman and Edmond Hall and Pee Wee Russell. His solos, whether embellishments of the melody or full-tilt improvisations, were faultlessly structured. He had a way of playing the melody that invariably suggested that *this* is the way it should sound. And he was right. If the melody had any excess weight, he eliminated a note here, a note there. If it was on the skinny side he added flourishes or moved down to the chalameau register, which tends to make every note sound treasured. He impressed his melodic approach so thoroughly on certain tunes that when they surface anew one automatically hears Shaw's rendition. *Vide Moonglow* and *Stardust* and *Dancing in the Dark*. Shaw's improvising was canny and agile. He used a great many notes, complex little runs that were almost asides, an on-the-beat attack, almost no vibrato, and soaring ascensions into the upper register. And he demonstrated considerable emotion on an instrument that resists it.[5]

Jerome Richardson, a notable jazz clarinetist, flautist, and saxophonist, has remarked:

> I was a Benny Goodman fan until I heard Artie Shaw, and that was it. He went places on the clarinet that no one had ever been before. He would get up to Bs and C's and make not notes but music, melodies. He must have worked out his own fingering for the high notes, because they weren't in the books. To draw a rough analogy, Artie Shaw was at that time [the 1930s and 40s] to clarinetists what Art Tatum was to pianists. It was another view of clarinet playing. A lot of people loved

Benny Goodman because it was within the scope of what most clarinet players could play and therefore could copy. But Artie Shaw took the instrument further.[6]

Saxophonist and clarinetist Bob Wilber believes that Shaw's playing had "a great lyric intensity. They say he worked out his solos beforehand. Certainly they are more like compositions than improvisations. He had a brilliant way of using sequential figures against the rhythm. He was very clever."[7]

Barney Bigard, the New Orleans clarinetist and long-serving member of Duke Ellington's orchestra, was—perhaps surprisingly, given their widely differing styles—also an ardent admirer of Shaw.

> What Shaw did to begin with was to make the clarinet sound unusually beautiful in the upper register. He wasn't a low-register guy, but he was more creative than Benny Goodman. Benny did all the popular tunes and standards, but Artie made up his own and played them so well. The guy could execute like mad. Benny could also execute, and had much more drive than Artie, but I like Artie for the things that were almost impossible to do on the clarinet.[8]

Shaw—as the sales of his records alone attest—had an enormous *popular* appeal in the 1930s and 40s, but aspiring jazz musicians of a younger generation than Bigard's also found in his playing much to engage their attention and admiration. Bop clarinetist Buddy DeFranco remembered that when he first heard Benny Goodman, "I was enthralled. He had fire *and* facility." But the young DeFranco had quickly switched his allegiance to Shaw. "He was more linear in his musical thinking than the arpeggiated Chicago players like Goodman. And he was more modern harmonically."[9] Altoist Paul Desmond, best-known for his recordings with the sensationally popular Dave Brubeck Quartet in the 1950s and 60s, recalled that as a high-school student in San Francisco in the late 1930s, his first instrument was the clarinet: "I was a real *clarinetnik*, I could play entire Artie Shaw choruses."[10] Bop trumpeter Benny Harris, in the course of a 1961 interview that appeared in *Metronome*, remembered that: "We listened to Artie Shaw instead of Benny Goodman. Goodman swung, but Shaw was more modern."[11]

Such estimates suggest that while Shaw might not have been perhaps the greatest jazzman ever to play the clarinet, he was certainly among the most gifted clarinetists ever to have played jazz. Unlike the majority of jazz clarinetists who elect to ignore the top register of the instrument, Shaw was perfectly at ease in this rarefied atmosphere. And, as he explained to Henry Duckham, a professional clarinetist and faculty member of the Oberlin Conservatory of Music in Ohio, this enviable ability grew directly out of conditions prevailing in the 1930s.

> My upper register developed from playing in front of a strong brass section when microphones weren't very good and large speakers didn't exist. I couldn't compete with trumpets playing high Ds and E-flats so I had to play high Gs and As and Bs and even Cs to get above them. In most clarinet literature there's no reason for that. I decided [that] if I were going to play up there it should sound like normal notes. I didn't see any reason for the tone to thin out. I worked at it. In front of my band you were playing in dance halls the size of Zeppelin hangars. There was only one microphone in front of the whole band.[12]

Along with Benny Goodman, Shaw was the virtuoso clarinetist of the Swing Era, and (like Goodman) was equally at ease
with the demands of classical composers for the instrument.
Shaw did not—either with his several orchestras or Gramercy
Fives—produce a body of recorded work that compares with that
of either Duke Ellington or Count Basie, the two pre-eminent
African-American orchestra leaders whose seminal contributions
to jazz both antedated and survived beyond the years of classic
big-band swing. But Shaw has every claim to be considered as
a great *innovator* of American popular music, not least for his
fascination and (not always successful) experiments with string
sections, and the inclusion of a harpsichord in the first edition of
the Gramercy Five.[13]

Albert McCarthy correctly observes that Shaw—despite or perhaps because of his constant changes of personnel—should be
considered as an exemplar of the best qualities of swing. His
great achievement

> was to prove that it was possible to organize a swing band that
> eschewed certain of the obvious conventions of the period, no-
> tably in showmanship and repertoire, and to succeed with a
> musical policy that was comparatively sophisticated. Shaw
> might not have been able to achieve all that he wished, but he
> did manage to produce a body of recordings in which musical
> values are paramount. In so doing, he triumphed more thor-
> oughly than perhaps he ever realized over the aspects of the
> music business which he so disliked.[14]

But it was with his small-group recordings, even more than
in his orchestral ventures, that Shaw most clearly demonstrated
a visceral feeling for jazz and improvisation. Vladimir Simosko, a

serious student of Shaw's Gramercy Five sessions, believes that they illustrate "a clear evolutionary tendency" in his playing from 1940 to 1954. The final Gramercy Five sessions, Simosko believes, "represent the culmination of his art as an instrumentalist and, to a certain extent, as a composer, in their treatment of old and new Shaw compositions." Simosko also makes the pertinent observation that

> It is instructive to compare these late Shaw items with the work of other major clarinetists in small group performances in the same period. Compared with the clarinet with rhythm and vibes recordings by Goodman, Shaw sounds polished, intellectual, and modern. Compared to the clarinet with rhythm performances of Buddy DeFranco or Tony Scott, Shaw sounds far more subtle and less boppish. The essential qualities of discipline and tightness in the performances Shaw produced become very obvious in this way.[15]

Always the complete musician, Shaw—unlike many of his contemporaries—sensed the limitations and restricted possibilities of conventional swing. From initially appearing to oppose the innovations of Dizzy Gillespie and Charlie Parker, Shaw—with more success than Benny Goodman, who had only a brief flirtation with the idiom—came to welcome and then to incorporate some of the complex musical vocabulary of bop into his last recorded work.

What is more difficult to gauge is the *meaning* which jazz (and swing-derived-from-jazz) had for Shaw. Gunther Schuller suggests that although jazz played an important part in Shaw's life, "it was a tenuous relationship, which could be broken at will. At times, jazz seemed for him only the *vehicle* by which he could dominate the music field and acquire the very fame which he then so very disdainfully decried in public." But of all the enigmas posed by Shaw's checkered career, Schuller believes that "the most profoundly perplexing one is how a true musician of his remarkable talents could so unconditionally leave music."[16]

Shaw himself has frequently been asked this question. Typical of his responses is this statement to George T. Simon in 1971:

> You see, music is such a horrendously all-consuming discipline. To play it up to the standards I had, I knew finally that I had to become such an overspecialized human being that there was nothing left for anything else. I just didn't want to become a half-assed human being in order to become a whole-assed musician. So I gave up.

More recently Shaw told Fred Hall that

> playing the way I demanded of myself required pretty much full-time commitment. And there was no time for anything else. I couldn't have any other kind of life. And finally I had a choice: playing and having the respect of your colleagues and making a lot of money and doing all of the things that go with success in show business is 40 per cent of a good life. Living is 60 per cent of a good life without music. So I'd have to opt for 60 as opposed to 40. But there's still 40 missing here. And I couldn't put the two together at the time. And by the time it became possible to put it together, to go out and play a series of 12 or 15 two-hour concerts and make enough for the year to support yourself so you could go on doing it the following year, I was, by that time, long gone from it. I'd gotten involved in literature and writing, and that was what I decided to do."[17]

In the same conversation, Shaw offered some thoughts on popular music in general and the Beatles in particular. Whereas Cole Porter, Lorenz Hart, Richard Rodgers, and Oscar Hammerstein had written musical compositions and lyrical poetry, the Beatles were responsible for *We All Live in a Yellow Submarine*— "hardly a musical statement."[18]

Asked for his opinion of the *rhythmic* element in the popular music of the 1970s, Shaw conceded that much of it had "energy and ferocity" yet quickly added a proviso and a historical dimension.

> But then, take the energy and ferocity of what was going on in the late thirties and early forties. That's hard to beat. It's hard to top what a Basie does or an Ellington at his peak. It's hard to top what I was doing at my peak, or what Benny was doing at his peak, or Tommy [Dorsey] at his. Take Jimmie Lunceford, that was a great band too.

Glenn Miller, Shaw pointedly observed, did not belong in this select company, since "musically, his was essentially ground-out music—ground-out like so many sausages." As for his *own* role as a bandleader, Shaw reflected that "I think the music I played was the best I could contrive to play, given what audiences would accept, given the length of records you had to make." Although his various orchestras had been playing in ballrooms, Shaw recalled that his concern had not been with *dancing*: "Our music was for listening primarily. Within the so-called dance format, we were playing concerts." In the halcyon years of Swing, this had been regarded as an eccentric idea. But, within a very few years "people finally got the idea that American jazz was a music *worth* listening to, that you didn't *have* to get up and dance."[19]

As mentioned, during his 1949 "Blindfold" test by critic Leonard Feather, Shaw had announced his admiration for Louis Armstrong. More recently, recalling his childhood in the 1920s, Shaw was more specific about Armstrong's influence and stature. "By the time you were old enough to appreciate Louis, you had been hearing those who derived from him. He defined not only how you play a trumpet solo but how you play a solo on any instrument." And he speculated that "had Louis Armstrong never lived, I suppose there would be jazz, but it would be very different."[20]

Invited by Chip Deffaa to name his first "musical influences," Shaw responded:

I think probably [Frank] Trumbauer and Bix [Beiderbecke], first. And then Louis. And then I went off to all the standard brands. Jimmy Noone, a few guys like that. There weren't too many people. I first heard Trumbauer and Bix on records. Then when they came nearby, when I was living in New Haven, I made a pilgrimage to Bridgeport one night. They were playing, the [Gene] Goldkette band came there [to] the Ritz ballroom, and I stood in front of that band open-mouthed. Then later I went to Harlem. And when I met Willie "The Lion" Smith, he was a big influence. Then I worked in radio with some fine musicians who weren't jazz players but I learned a lot about breathing and tone control and discipline in playing.[21]

Other jazz performers who have received Shaw's stamp of approval include the pianists Art Tatum and Hank Jones, tenor/

alto saxophonist/clarinetist Art Pepper, altoists Julian "Cannon-
ball" Adderley and Lee Konitz, and tenor saxophonist/clarinetist
Lester Young. In a 1984 interview with Loren Schoenberg, Shaw
spoke of his admiration for Young's tenor playing. Recalling his
friendship with Young in the 1930s, when they frequently
jammed together, Shaw remarked that "Lester had more of an
effect on me than any clarinetist" and extolled one particular aspect of Young's style:

> Lester played very, very relaxedly; he wasn't pushing the beat.
> If anything, he was lagging behind. This was not done at that
> time. His ability to handle eighth notes without rushing them
> was beautiful. Also, Lester played *music* first, jazz second.
> When Lester played something, and I would follow him, we
> were kind of meshing. It was a very interesting kind of juxtapo-
> sition of two quite different sensibilities doing almost identi-
> cally the same thing.[22]

In 1992, Shaw permitted the release of private recordings of
his 1954 Gramercy Five on CD (see chapter 7). Reviewing these
"Final Sessions," *New York Times* critic John S. Wilson found
much to commend. He also offered an informed perspective on
Shaw's post-World War II career—and the public's response:

> Unlike his band-leading peers in the Swing Era—Tommy Dor-
> sey, Benny Goodman, Glenn Miller—Mr. Shaw was stimu-
> lated by the new jazz called be-bop that cropped up in the
> 1940s. He began incorporating bop musicians in his band
> [and] his own clarinet playing became coloured with bop
> ideas. His old fans, like most swing band fans, resented bop
> and were not prepared to accept his new approaches. When
> he felt that his 1954 Gramercy Five was so good that its work

deserved to be preserved, but no record company was interested, he took the group, morning after morning, into a recording studio at 5 a.m. after a night's work at the Embers and recorded its entire "book."

The 1954 Gramercy Five sessions, Wilson suggested, prompted the thought that Shaw had quit the music business prematurely, just as "a new kind of combo jazz"—represented by The Modern Jazz Quartet and baritone saxophonist Gerry Mulligan's celebrated quartets—was about to capture a wide audience. In effect, Shaw had been "a bridge between the Swing Era and these 1950s groups," and had he delayed his retirement, might have discovered "many of his old friends who had not adjusted to his new moves primarily because it was he who made them, waiting for him in the jazz atmosphere that . . . Mulligan and the Modern Jazz Quartet and others created in the mid-50's."[23]

The same critic hailed Shaw's return to fronting a big band in 1983. At seventy-three years of age, Shaw was "trim, tanned and vigorous, bald with a fringe of greying hair and a grey moustache." Conducting a newly formed Artie Shaw Orchestra, with the clarinet parts played by Dick Johnson, Shaw was quoted as saying: "I feel like I'm coming down in a flaming chariot like an icon. I haven't wanted to play for 30 years but now I'm really turned on. This band is doing things after only two weeks that my old band struggled with for six months. Ultimately, I hope to get my band to sound as though it had continued from where I left and had gone on into the 1980s." Performing a mixture of updated arrangements of such 1940s hits as *Traffic Jam* and *Dancing in the Dark*, Shaw was also introducing new material, like Miles Davis's *Milestones*. But this was an Artie Shaw Or-

chestra in name only. Shaw called Dick Johnson "the best clarinetist I've ever heard," but added that "he's in an impossible
position. He's trying to be me, and he can't be himself."[24]

An irascible and quixotic survivor of the Swing Era, Artie
Shaw was one of its most gifted performers, and led one of the
best white swing aggregations.[25] He also remains swing's most
intriguing figure, at once its most gifted and miserable participant, most anguished critic, and unabashed latter-day celebrant.
If and when it is finally completed, *The Education of Albie Snow*
should provide a fuller understanding of the troubles and tri-
umphs of Arthur Arshawsky and his alter ego Artie Shaw. Until
then, newcomers to his *music* might well *Begin* (with) the *Beguine*, *Summit Ridge Drive*, *Frenesi*, and *Stardust*—or any of the
Shavian confections and delights discussed in the next chapter.

NOTES

1. "Homage to Artie Shaw," *The Clarinet* 14 (Summer 1987), 32.

2. Gene Lees, *Meet Me At Jim & Andy's*, 60.

3. John McDonough, "Artie Shaw: Non-stop Flight from 1938,"
Down Beat, 37 (January 22, 1970), 13. *The Swing Era*, 693.

4. Richard Palmer and John White, eds., *Larkin's Jazz: Essays and
Reviews 1940–1984 (London and New York: Continuum, 2001).* 79.

5. *New York Notes*, 107.

6. Lees, *Meet Me at Jim & Andy's*, 60.

7. Whitney Balliett, *American Musicians: 56 Portraits in Jazz* (New
York and Oxford: Oxford University Press, 1986), 60.

8. Stanley Dance, *The World of Duke Ellington* (New York: Charles
Scribner's Sons, 1970). 88

9. Balliett, *Barney, Bradley, and Max*. 198.

10. Joe Goldberg, *Jazz Masters of the Fifties* (London: Collier-Macmillan, 1965), 156.

11. Albert J. McCarthy. Sleeve note to *Artie Shaw: Concerto for Clarinet* (RCA Records, 1972).

12. Henry Duckham, "A Masterclass with Artie Shaw," *The Clarinet*, 12 (1985), 13.

13. Jazz critics have generally deplored the magnetic attraction of string sections to such major performers as Stan Getz, Billie Holiday, Sarah Vaughan, Charlie Parker, Art Pepper, Clifford Brown, and Wynton Marsalis—yet they have all produced some of their finest work in these surroundings.

14. *Big Band Jazz*, 265.

15. Vladimir Simosko, "Artie Shaw and his Gramercy Fives," *Journal of Jazz Studies*, 1, No. 1 (October 1973), 51. In conversation with Simosko (and before the release of all of these "last recordings"), Shaw commented: "They contain the best playing I ever did. We would go down to my house after work and really stretch out. We did reinterpretations of tunes like *Begin the Beguine* and *Stardust*, but in a more contemporary style, and originals that never got on record like *Overdrive*, but they could never be released by commercial recording companies. They aren't interested in little subtleties that make a better performance; they want something that will sell." 49.

16. *The Swing Era*, 714. Shaw himself, obviously stung by Schuller's rhetorical question, has commented that: "Schuller couldn't figure out why I quit. My God, I've said it enough times. He's telling me more about himself, like 'if I'd had that kind of success I'd never have quit.' That's what comes out between the lines." Notes to "Artie Shaw: The Last Recordings: Rare & Unreleased." Musicmasters Jazz CD (Ocean: New Jersey, 1992).

17. *The Big Bands*, 548. *Dialogues in Swing*, 142–3.

18. *Ibid.* 549–50. Philip Larkin takes an analogous view of the Beatles' later offerings. Reviewing the record "A Collection of Beatles Oldies" in 1967, he typified it as "more a short history of this musical phenomenon from *She Loves You* to *Eleanor Rigby* [that] would prove admirable demonstration material for Marx's theory of artistic degener-

ation: WEA lecturers please note." *All What Jazz*, 178. In an earlier notice of the album *With the Beatles*, Larkin suggested that "their jazz content is nil, but like certain sweets, they seem wonderful until you are suddenly sick." *Ibid*. 102.

19. *The Big Bands*, 547. Shaw gave a similar answer to Chip Deffaa when asked what bands he most admired. "I liked Ellington, when he was good, when he was real good. But he never had much of an influence, musically, on bands . . . I'm talking about an overall influence. Basie had an influence. I had an influence. Benny had an influence. Even Tommy Dorsey had an influence at his best, because Tommy was a fine musician and he insisted on perfection in that band. And they gave him that. Very close to it. The only thing is, he got into singers. When you get into singers, you're in the entertainment business." *Swing Legacy*. 33.

20. *Meet Me at Jim & Andy's*, 70.

21. *Swing Legacy*, 21.

22. Loren Schoenberg. Liner notes to Musicmasters CD *"Artie Shaw and his Orchestra: 1949: Previously Unreleased Recordings"* (Ocean, New Jersey, 1990). After his discharge from the Navy, Shaw sat in with the Count Basie orchestra when it was appearing at the Plantation Ballroom in the Watts section of Los Angles. On these occasions, Shaw traded clarinet breaks with Lester Young (soon to be drafted into the US Army). After Young's induction, Shaw would play Young's tenor parts on the clarinet. In a later conversation with Schoenberg, Shaw remarked that he had not been influenced only by horn players: "I think I learned as much from Earl Hines as I did from Louis [Armstrong], and I learned as much from Art Tatum as I did from any clarinet player." Liner notes to *Artie Shaw: More Last Recordings: The Final Sessions* (Jazz Heritage CD 52344F: Ocean, New Jersey: Musical Heritage Society, Inc., 1993), 9.

23. John S. Wilson, "Artie Shaw Rarities Come to Light," *New York Times*, (no date),1984. Shaw File. Institute of Jazz Studies.

24. John S. Wilson, "Artie Shaw Returns at 73," *New York Times*, December 19, 1983.

25. Whitney Balliett endorses this verdict, but also poses and answers the question: "What, after all were the others like? Glenn Miller's

band, with its bosomy reed voicings and high-heeled rhythm section, had a feminine air, as did Harry James's band, which was dominated by his divalike trumpet. Jimmy Dorsey's band was bland and buttery, while his brother's veered back and forth between *Walpurgisnacht* and moonsville. . . . Jan Savitt and Glen Gray operated well-oiled pumps, and so did Benny Goodman, except for that brief, green time in the summer of 1941 when he had Cootie Williams and Mel Powell and Charlie Christian and Sid Catlett." *New York Notes*, 106. (Curiously, Balliett leaves Woody Herman out of his reckoning.)

'S Wonderful: Artie Shaw on Record

I created a piece of Americana that is going to go on and on—whether I'm here or not.

Artie Shaw

A number of celebrity "castaways" on the long-running BBC radio program "Desert Island Discs" have chosen recordings by Artie Shaw to lighten their solitude. These declared Shavians included tennis player Tony Mottram (*Frenesi*), comedians Tony Hancock (*Gloomy Sunday*) and Eric Morecambe and Ernie Wise (*Begin the Beguine*), arranger Nelson Riddle (*Frenesi*), singers Bing Crosby (*Begin the Beguine*) and Mel Tormé (*The Carioca*), and actor-director Mel Brooks (*Begin the Beguine*). Asked in 1979 on a California radio station to select his *own* desert island discs, Shaw—after some hesitation—selected *The Maid With the Flaccid Hair*, an Eddie Sauter composition, adapting the title of Debussy's *Maid With the Flaccid Air*, recorded by Shaw in 1944, and the composer Paul Jordan's *Suite No. 8*, a Shaw recording of 1942.

Artie Shaw is well represented in the current record catalogues, and reissues of his various orchestras and small groups are increasingly available on CD compilations. The following items—forming only a small part of his oeuvre—are offered as suggested (and rewarding) listening.

ANTHOLOGIES

Artie Shaw: Non-Stop Flight, (Jazz CD 016) in the *Jazz Greats* series (Marshall Cavendish Partworks Limited, 1996) is an excellently re-mastered collection of Shaw big-band and small-group recordings from 1938 to 1941. Titles include *Any Old Time, Stardust, Begin the Beguine, Nightmare, Frenesi,* and *Concerto for Clarinet*. More readily available—and even more enticing—is **Artie Shaw: The Classic Tracks** (KAZ CD 305), a superb compilation of studio recordings (1937–1940) which includes—in addition to many of the titles on **Artie Shaw: Non-Stop Flight**—both *The Blues March,* Parts 1 & 2 (1937), and *The Blues,* Parts 1 & 2 (1940).[1] **Artie Shaw: Stardust** (Hallmark CD 306672) and **"Gloomy Sunday": Artie Shaw and His Orchestra 1938–1941** (Jazz Roots CD 56003) are inexpensive and also worth acquiring, as is **A Jazz Hour With the Artie Shaw Orchestra: Indian Love Call** (JHR 73565), all 1938 recordings.

Pride of place goes to **Self Portrait** (Bluebird 09026-63808-25CD), a five-CD set of ninety-five titles selected by Shaw himself. It is the most representative collection to date of his oeuvre, with studio and live recordings from 1936 to 1954. The impressive accompanying booklet includes Shaw's (alternately modest and boastful) comments on his selections in conversation with Richard Sudhalter.

THE EARLY YEARS

The young Artie Shaw can be heard to good effect on four Billie Holiday studio sessions recorded in July, 1936 (*The Quintessential Billie Holiday: Volume 2*, Columbia CD, CK 40790), in the distinguished company of Bunny Berigan (trumpet), Joe Bushkin (piano), Dick McDonough (guitar), Pete Peterson (bass), and Cozy Cole (drums). On *Did I Remember? No Regrets* and *Summertime*, Shaw plays competent if unremarkable accompaniments, but on *Billie's Blues* he delivers a fine blues-drenched solo—as does Berigan. Shaw was also present at the session which produced the first (1936) Berigan version of *I Can't Get Started With You*, contained on *Bunny Berigan and The Rhythm Makers: Volume 1*, (Jass J-CD 627).

The famous Shaw string quartet and rhythm section performance of *Interlude in B Flat*, given at the Imperial Theater in New York City in 1936, can be found with some application (but in poor sound quality) on *Artie Shaw: A Legacy* (Book-of-the-Month Records: 1984). Richard Sudhalter suggests that this version of *Interlude* was, in fact, a studio—rather than a "live"—recording. Shaw himself is unsure: "I must have taken the group into a studio, perhaps right afterwards, and recorded it. But I don't remember doing that."[2]

This eight-volume LP special edition set (yet to be issued on CD) also includes Shaw's appearance with Paul Whiteman's

Orchestra at Carnegie Hall on Christmas Day, 1938, in a ravishing and extended solo on *The Blues*. Shaw has commented on his performance of *The Blues*:

> This wasn't rehearsed. Paul Whiteman asked me if I'd appear on his annual Christmas concert as a guest soloist. I said I could appear, but I couldn't possibly find time to rehearse. I said, "Give me Ferde Grofe or Bill Challis or one of your other arrangers, and I'll dictate a framework and they can write it out." I think the arranger he gave me was Irving Szathmary, a Hungarian with a fair knowledge of jazz who had joined Whiteman to write for that big orchestra of his. You'll notice a point where I go up to a high G and go bop-bop-bop, four beats to a bar, for a few bars. I did it because the orchestra, not being an organized jazz band, was not too with it when it came to hitting a beat. I decided it was time to settle them down a little. You'll notice I'm almost *behind* the beat, slowing them down, getting them to stop rushing.[3]

Richard Sudhalter comments that this "lengthy essay" on the blues, played at various tempos, included "a long cantorial central cadenza section, a paraphrase of *St. Louis Blues* and a clarinet-and-tom-tom episode faintly reminiscent of [Benny] Goodman's *Sing Sing Sing* party piece," culminating on "a preternaturally high C." But the most amazing aspect of this bravura performance was the fact that Shaw sustains the listener's interest for nearly eleven-and-a-half minutes. "There are scarcely four bars anywhere in this performance when he is *not* playing. It is all Shaw."[4] Arguably Shaw's finest recorded solo, it needs to be reissued in a digitally re-mastered version.

The Book-of-the Month set also contains Shaw's perform-ances of Mozart's *Clarinet Quintet in A Major, K. 581*, and Kr-ein's *Hebrew Sketches, No.2*, op.*13*, with the WOR studio's string quartet from a radio broadcast of 1947, and Berezowsky's *Con-certo for Clarinet and Orchestra in B-Flat*, op.28, recorded at Car-negie Hall in 1948 with Leon Barzin and the National Youth Symphony.[5]

Studio recordings by Shaw's first orchestras are on ***Thou Swell: Artie Shaw and His Orchestra*** (Living Era LP, AJA 5056, also available with additional tracks on CD). Titles include *Shoot the Likker To Me, John Boy, All Alone, Blue Skies, The Chant*, and *Thou Swell*. Apart from Shaw himself, trumpeter John Best and drummer Cliff Leeman are the outstanding musi-cians on these sessions (with various personnels) of 1936–1937. An older LP compilation, ***Free For All*** (CBS Realm 52636), produced by Frank Driggs, is worth looking for in specialist shops. An anthology of Shaw's 1937 recordings for Brunswick, it contains such essential items as *All Alone, Night and Day, Night-mare, Free for All, Non-Stop Flight*, and *The Blues*: Parts 1 and 2. (Reviewing this record on its release in 1969, Philip Larkin noted: "It's entertaining to note how drummer Cliff Leeman bought a cymbal halfway through the year that sounded like a metallic sneeze, and couldn't leave it alone").[6]

Artie Shaw and His Orchestra 1938 (Le Jazz CD 8108) covers a seminal year in Shaw's career, with the release of *Begin the Beguine* and *Indian Love Call*, and contains nineteen other studio recordings.

Broadcasts by the Shaw orchestra of 1938–1939 have been collected on three Hindsight CDs, ***King of the Clarinet***

1938–39 (HBCD—502). Jerry Gray or Shaw himself arranged most of the titles, and the personnel includes George Auld, Les Robinson, and Tony Pastor (saxophones), Les Jenkins and George Arus (trombones), Bernie Privin and Chuck Peterson (trumpets), Bob Kitsis (piano), Sid Weiss (bass), and Buddy Rich (drums). Vocals are by the mediocre Pastor and the excellent Helen Forrest. These "airshots" also offer interesting and instructive comparisons with studio versions of the same titles. A single-volume anthology of these broadcasts is contained on *Artie Shaw and His Orchestra: 22 Originals From 1938–1939* (Hindsight HCD 401), with a generous playing time of nearly one and one-half hours. Buddy Rich can clearly be heard exhorting the band in a storming performance of *Carioca*, and there are spirited renditions of *Shine on Harvest Moon, My Heart Stood Still, What Is This Thing Called Love*, and (improbably) *The Lambeth Walk*. Listening to these selections, Shaw has commented on their "spontaneity" and daring, in comparison with studio sessions of the period when "there was no tape and you knew you were going to have to be perfect. The tension got very high [and] often you wouldn't take chances on doing things that might go wrong."

THE RCA YEARS

Shaw's most renowned—and arguably his finest—orchestral and small-group recordings were those produced by the RCA Company from 1938 to 1945. As Eric Thacker observes of the big-band sessions: "The embracing vision is Shaw's own. He is a

tutelary spirit combining Prospero and Ariel in one, and his writers must often have been expressing his concepts at least as
much as their own. As a player, his range of ideas is not wide,
but with a tone squeezed from the blues into affective sounds
and an intense, almost harrowing, attenuation in upper registers,
and with a facility of technique saved from glibness by the fine
excitement of his constantly soaring melodies, he gives the band
much of its distinction."[7] These astute comments are borne out
on **Begin the Beguine: Artie Shaw and His Orchestra** (RCA
Bluebird ND 82432), which contains the title track plus *Traffic
Jam, Back Bay Shuffle, What Is This Thing Called Love, Indian
Love Call* (featuring a Shaw trademark—a duet between tom-
toms and clarinet), *Deep Purple, Moon Ray, Carioca,* and other
classics. The informative sleeve note is by Chris Albertson.
**Blues in the Night: Artie Shaw and His Orchestra featur-
ing Roy Eldridge and "Hot Lips" Page** (RCA Bluebird ND
82432) is a welcome compilation of 1941–1945 sessions spot-
lighting Shaw's two great African-American trumpet players.
Page is featured prominently on *St. James Infirmary* and *Blues in
the Night,* while Eldridge shines and dazzles on *Little Jazz* and
Lady Day. This CD also has performances of scores by Eddie
Sauter (*Summertime* and *They Didn't Believe Me*) and Paul Jordan (*Suite No. 8, Carnival,* and *Two in One Blues*). Dan Morgenstern's accompanying essay is perceptive and instructive.

    Artie Shaw: The Complete Gramercy Five Sessions
(RCA Bluebird ND 87637) features two editions of Shaw's famous small group, with Johnny Guarnieri's harpsichord or Dodo
Marmarosa's piano lending some "ancient" and "modern" bounce
to the respective proceedings. Both groups sound surprisingly

fresh and animated, with the instruments juxtaposed in an engaging variety of combinations and shades of emphasis. Trumpeters Roy Eldridge and Billy Butterfield make their own sterling and idiosyncratic contributions. *When the Quail Come Back to San Quentin, Scuttlebutt, Mysterioso* (two takes), and *Smoke Gets in Your Eyes* are among the other titles. Needless to say, the leader's clarinet is polished, immaculate, and exhilaratingly agile on both sessions (1940 and 1945).

In the Blue Room/In The Cafe Rouge (RCA Victor 74321 18527–2) are CD versions (in very acceptable sound quality) of 1938/39 performances (with a short spoken introduction by Shaw, recorded in the 1950s for the LP issue). On both dates, the band plays its hit charts with great enthusiasm, and Shaw, rising to the occasion(s), offers some biting and characteristically lucid solos.

Artie Shaw and His Orchestra 1944–45 (Hep CD 70) is a splendid three-volume set of recordings made in New York City and Hollywood for the Victor and Musicraft labels. It includes such Shavian gems as *'S Wonderful, Summertime, The Maid With the Flaccid Air, September Song, Bedford Drive,* and *Grabtown Grapple.* There are also exhilarating "Jubilee" radio broadcast performances by Shaw with the Count Basie Orchestra (*Lady Be Good* and *Artie's Blues*), and a Gramercy Five Kraft Music Hall appearance with Bing Crosby (*I Was Doing All Right* and *You Took Advantage of Me*).

LATER RECORDINGS

Artie Shaw and His Orchestra: 1949 (Musicmasters CD CIJD6 0234 M and Cassette CIJD4 0234 T) are previously unreleased recordings by Shaw's most "progressive" and adventurous aggregation. The distinguished personnel include Al Cohn and Zoot Sims (tenors), Herb Stewart (alto), Don Fagerquist (trumpet), Fred Zito (trombone), and Irv Kluger (drums). Shaw says of his clarinet playing on these sessions: "My whole sound and approach to playing had changed. It got pure, and a little more refined. Instead of a vibrato, I tried to get a ripple." The exceptional results can be heard on updated versions of *Stardust* (where Fred Zito recreates Jack Jenney's original solo), *'S Wonderful* and such originals as *Krazy Kat* (arranged by Johnny Mandel), *Fred's Delight*, and *So Easy* (arranged by Tad Dameron and Shaw).

The critically underrated (with one notable exception) 1954/55 Gramercy Five studio sessions are now available in their entirety as **Artie Shaw: *The Last Recordings*** (Musicmasters CD 65701-2) and **More Last Recordings: *The Final Sessions*** (Music Masters and Jazz Heritage 52344F). Available earlier only on abridged Verve and Book-of-the-Month Club compilations, they are revelatory latter day examples of Shaw's artistry, inventiveness, and humor. Shaw has remarked that these "last recordings" contain "the best playing I ever did." On all the tracks, he sounds totally involved and supremely confident. As he recalled: "I hadn't played for about a year and a half when I made these records, but I had been listening a lot. When I put this group together I wanted to work with modern players." The (distinguished) "modern players" were Hank Jones (piano), Tal Farlow or Joe Puma (guitar), Tommy Potter (bass), and Irv Kluger (drums). Among other things, these recordings show—as Dan Morgenstern notes—that Shaw had (finally) "retired at the height of his powers." His playing on both of these (double) CD sets, delicately balanced between the poles of swing and bop, is remarkably lithe. There are extended performances of familiar titles in the Shavian lexicon—*When the Quail Come Back to San Quentin, Begin the Beguine, Stardust, Frenesi, Grabtown Grapple*—together with less well-known Shaw originals—*Stop and Go Mambo, Lugubrious,* and *The Chaser,* together with standards like *Imagination, How High the Moon,* and *Tenderly.* Every track contains its own delights and revelations, and it would be invidious to single out a particular performance. Suffice it to say that in the company of sympathetic and accomplished sidemen, these "last recordings" are essential items in the Shaw discography. Like the best of small-group swing/jazz, they offer inventiveness, intelligence, involvement, rhythm, and (not least) rapture. Ironically, they also suggest that Shaw was perhaps at the height of his powers as an improviser on the eve of his (final) retirement.

In an appreciative and incisive review of these sessions, critic Gary Giddins asserted that "they are among the finest performances by one of the eminent clarinetists of the [twentieth] century" and are to be considered as "among the most enchanting small band recordings in jazz history, virtually unrivaled in defining the nexus between swing and bop."

> The music is romantic, daring, and exquisitely played—it doesn't sound like that of any other small band of the era. Nowhere does one sense the slightest tension between players or styles. [Hank] Jones has never sounded more liltingly attentive; [Tal] Farlow is fleet and witting; [Joe] Roland is percussively sure; and [Tommy] Potter is an oak.

But it is Shaw who receives the greatest praise for what were perhaps his greatest performances on the clarinet.

The first thing that grabs you is his sound, which is almost ethereal; the next thing is his breath control. His phrases aren't merely long, but cannily long—always pressing for one more detail, one more turn, rarely content to fold into the eight-bar phrases of the songs themselves. For the first time in Shaw's career, at the very moment it ended, we hear him disporting himself in expansive play. Even his quotations have an air of inspiration.[8]

NOTES

1. Balliett observes of this five-and-a-half minute performance that "Shaw excepted [it] is a funny and rather touching instance of white boys trying to play those low-down Negro blues." *New York Notes*, 108.

2. *Lost Chords*, 820, Note 15.

3. Booklet with *Artie Shaw: A Legacy*, (Camp Hill, Pennsylvania: Book-of-the-Month Club, Inc., 1984), 14.

4. *Lost Chords*, 587.

5. On Mozart's *Clarinet Quintet* Shaw employs vibrato. Asked by other clarinet players why he had adopted this unconventional approach to the piece, he retorted: "Why shouldn't the clarinet use vibrato? Why should it come out sounding like a miniature foghorn playing with the strings?" and adds pertinently: "Vibrato is simply a way of embellishing tone. You can play the instrument dead or with some embellishment." Shaw recalled of this performance of Berezowsky's composition: "The first movement baffled the audience totally. But by the second movement they apparently began to understand that there was also humor in the piece, and at the end of that movement they finally unbent enough to laugh. The last movement is one of the toughest things I have ever played on the clarinet. There's one segment of ten or eleven seconds that I spent almost three months practicing." *Artie Shaw: A Legacy*, 13.

6. *All What Jazz*, 227.

7. Max Harrison, Charles Fox and Eric Thacker, The Essential Jazz Records: Volume I, Ragtime to Swing (London: Mansell Publishing, 1984), 331.

8. Giddins, *Visions of Jazz*, "'Artie Shaw (Cinderella's Last Stand)," 204, 208–09.

Shaw, London, 1949

CODA

The Best of Intentions

Go away

Artie Shaw: Revised Epitaph for *Who's Who In America*

All Artie ever wanted was for you to tell him how good he was,
or more, how much better he was than Benny.

Johnny Guarnieri

In 1992, the American clarinetist and saxophonist Bob Wilber—now living in England—persuaded Shaw (a few days after his eighty-second birthday) to conduct a concert at the Royal Festival Hall, performed by the Wren Orchestra and a small jazz combo. The program included Shaw's own composition *Concerto for Clarinet*, recreations of his Gramercy Five recordings, and Prokofiev's *Classical Symphony*. An admirer of Shaw's *Concerto for Clarinet*, Wilber observed in a newspaper interview that "it has a cadenza that starts climbing from concert double-F and slides through every note up to high B-flat which is quite stratospheric for the clarinet." He also singled out the 1940 version of *Stardust* as a superb example of musical *construction*: "You could put that solo on paper and it would attract anyone who had never heard him play it."[1]

Shaw's conducting appearance in London saw a flurry of newspaper articles and interviews that offered some pertinent facts about and comments on his life and times. *Guardian* readers were informed that Artie Shaw "has been described by those who admire him as a stickler for discipline, outspoken, hotheaded and cantankerous." Those who might never have heard of (let alone *heard*) Shaw were told that he was "the New-York born musician [who] had rocketed to fame during the swing era as a bandleader idol of bobbysoxers and jitterbugs."[2]

Stephen Pile, journalist for the *Sunday Telegraph*, had visited Shaw at his Newbury Park home in California, shortly before his departure for the London concert. "A lot of people," Pile reported "think [that] Artie Shaw has been dead for years. In fact, this jazz legend, clarinetist and bandleader of the Forties simply stepped out of the limelight in 1954."

During a four-hour interview, Pile asked the "jazz legend" about his many marriages, and received a gnomic (or self-justifying) reply.

> None of them were real marriages. They were legalised affairs. In those days you couldn't get a lease on an apartment if you were living in sin. People ask me why I married Ava Gardner. Did you ever *see* Ava Gardner? When a ravishing woman comes up and says she has always adored my work, what do you expect me to do? I had no choice but to marry her.

Shaw also offered another (not entirely convincing) explanation of his decision to leave the music business in 1939. "My own musical development and public taste coincided for a brief period at the end of the Thirties. After that, public taste stayed the same and I went on developing. But they wouldn't let me do it. They paid me millions to go on playing the same tunes."

Concerning his celebrated search for musical perfection, Shaw claimed: "I only hit what I wanted on a clarinet once in 30 years. It was a cadenza at the end of the old Decca recording of *These Foolish Things*. The band came to a stop and I improvised something that takes people six months to learn. It sounds like a composed piece." Asked by another interviewer to select his favorite solo, Shaw replied: "There are about 11 bars that I played that are about perfect, or about as close to perfection as you can get. They are the 11 bars or the cadenza at the end of *These Foolish Things*—that isn't even in print any more. It's remarkable clarinet, you can't do better. If anybody did it as well, it wouldn't be better because [they would be] copying me."[3]

Artie Shaw, as his most severe (and occasionally spiteful) critic Gunther Schuller concludes, was "compelled with an all-consuming passion to prove that he could play the clarinet better than anyone else." A lifelong and often frantic searcher for a musical *identity*, Shaw despite his protestations to the contrary, was "at heart a populist" who "could rarely resist the temptations to commercialize his talents, thereby undermining the best that was in him as a creative musician." Yet he "was able in his *finest* accomplishments to sweep us along in his searchings and discoveries and at one point (1939) represent the best the Swing Era had to offer."[4] As Shaw himself not immodestly informed journalist Joe Smith: "I was the biggest thing there was. I was doing fine, but I didn't like the life. There were six of us who made that era—Dorsey, Goodman, me, Miller, Lunceford, and Basie. All of them are dead, and here I am. I must have done something right."[5]

Shaw's longevity is to be welcomed, but his cavalier omissions of Duke Ellington, Fletcher Henderson, and drummer-leader Chick Webb from the roster of stellar contributors to the Swing Era are both curious and perverse. Ellington's 1942 orchestra not only assimilated everything Swing had meant, it also enriched and extended the genre. As one of Ellington's biographers asserts: "The Duke Ellington orchestra predated the swing craze by a decade, helped in fact to foster it, popularized its catch phrase [*It Don't Mean a Thing If It Ain't Got That Swing*], and provided its highest benchmarks of originality."[6]

In a 1992 interview, Shaw recalled that Ellington had once told him that "he was tired of the problems of leading a band, and that he [had] kept it going because it was the only way to hear his compositions."[7] As has been seen, Shaw was never wholly dedicated to a life in music. Consequently, his achievements as a bandleader are neither as consistent or as impressive as those of Duke Ellington, Count Basie, Benny Goodman, or Woody Herman.

Yet Shaw also achieved greatness in his clarinet playing. Not least—and unusually for a *white* musician—he had real empathy with the blues, the taproot of jazz. Asked in a recent radio profile to account for this feeling and facility, Shaw remarked: "My background was Russian Jewish. I think blues has a great deal of affinity with the Jewish experience—as it did with the black experience. A minority group is very hip to what the blues are about."

Given his introspective nature, volatile temperament, and eclectic interests, Shaw's "non-stop flight" in the perilous worlds of American jazz, swing, and popular music was always a hazardous as well as a romantic adventure—not unlike that of the eponymous heroine of *Cinderella*. But unlike that decidedly feminine, yet unfeminist, creature who achieved success by marrying her prince and living happily ever after, the more perceptive Shaw found that "$ucce$$"—at least in an unashamedly capitalist society—brought its own penalties. In his liner-note comments on the performances contained in the five-CD set "Artie Shaw-Self Portrait" (see chapter 7), Shaw reflects: "The big problem for some people—and unfortunately I'm one of them—is that you eventually reach a point where you're never satisfied with what you're doing. You finally get to where good enough ain't good enough. It's as if someone had laid a curse on you. I was never satisfied." Surveying his checkered career(s), self-justifying rationales, and current iconic status, one is drawn to Richard Sudhalter's verdict that despite "the best of intentions" the troubled Shaw himself was (and remains) "his own trouble with Cinderella."[8]

NOTES

1. Ronald Atkins, "Hot Head Comes Back on a High Note," *The Guardian*, June 11, 1992.

2. *Ibid*.

3. Sheila Tracy, *Bands, Booze And Broads* (Edinburgh and London: Mainstream Publishing, 1995), 237–8. See also: Henry Duckham, "Artie Shaw's Cadenza from *These Foolish Things*," *The Clarinet*, (Summer, 1987), 33.

4. *The Swing Era*, 714.

5. *Off the Record*, 22.

6. John Edward Hasse, *Beyond Category: The Life and Genius of Duke Ellington* (New York: Simon and Schuster, 1993), 202. Hasse emphasises this point: "Ellington's music exceeded the conventions, accomplishments, and boundaries of swing." 203. Scott Yanow observes that Count Basie and Duke Ellington "were satisfied to lead just one orchestra during the swing era, and Benny Goodman (due to illness) had two." Artie Shaw led *five*, although "all of them were distinctive and memorable." Michael Erlewine et al., eds. *All Music Guide to Jazz* (San Francisco: Miller Freeman Books, 1996), 652.

7. Hasse, *Beyond Category*, 357.

8. *Lost Chords*, 619.

Swing Survivor

SELECT
BIBLIOGRAPHY

Allen, Frederick Lewis. *Since Yesterday* (New York: Bantam Books, 1961).

Balliett, Whitney. *American Musicians: 56 Portraits in Jazz* (New York & Oxford: Oxford University Press, 1986).

———. *Barney, Bradley, & Max: 16 Portraits in Jazz* (New York: Oxford University Press, 1986).

———. *Goodbyes And Other Messages: A Journal of Jazz, 1981–1990* (New York and Oxford: Oxford University Press, 1991).

———. *New York Notes: A Journal of Jazz in the Seventies* (Boston: Houghton Mifflin Company, 1976).

———. *Night Creature: A Journal of Jazz, 1975–1980* (New York: Oxford University Press, 1981).

Blandford, Edmund L. *Artie Shaw: A Bio-Discography* (Hastings, Sussex: Castle Books, 1973).

———. "Artie Shaw and his US Navy 'Rangers' Band," *Jazz Journal International*, 51 (March 1998)), 6–11.

Charters, Samuel B. and Leonard Kunstadt. *Jazz: A History of the New York Scene* (New York: Da Capo Press, 1981).

Chilton, John. *Billie's Blues* (London: Quartet Books, 1975).

Clarke, Donald. *Wishing on the Moon: The Life and Times of Billie Holiday* (New York: Viking Books, 1994).

Collier, James Lincoln. *Benny Goodman and the Swing Era* (New York and Oxford: Oxford University Press, 1990).

———. *The Making of Jazz: A Comprehensive History* (London: Macmillan, 1981).

Cook, Richard and Brian Morton. *The Penguin Guide to Jazz on CD*, 6th edition (London and New York: Penguin Books, 2002).

Condon, Eddie and Richard Gehman. *Eddie Condon's Treasury of Jazz* (New York: Dial Press, 1956).

Crowther, Bruce. *Benny Goodman* (London: Apollo Press, 1988).

Crowther, Bruce and Mike Pinfold. *The Big Band Years* (London: David and Charles, 1988).

Dance, Stanley. *The World of Duke Ellington* (New York: Charles Scribner's Sons, 1970).

———. *The World of Swing* (New York: Charles Scribner's Sons, 1974).

———. *Jazz Era: the 'Forties* (London: MacGibbon and Kee, 1961).

Deffaa, Chip. *Swing Legacy* (Metuchen, New Jersey: Scarecrow Press and Institute of Jazz Studies, Rutgers University, 1989).

DeVeaux, Scott. *The Birth of Bebop: A Social and Musical History* (Berkeley, Los Angeles and London: University of California Press, 1997).

Duckham, Henry. "A Masterclass With Artie Shaw," *The Clarinet* 12 (1985), 10–16.

Ellington, Duke. *Music Is My Mistress* (New York: Doubleday, 1973).

Erenberg, Lewis A. "Things to Come: Swing Bands, Bebop, and the Rise of the Postwar Jazz Scene," in Larry May, ed., *Recasting America: Culture and Politics in the Age of the Cold War* (Chicago and London: University of Chicago Press, 1989).

———. *Swinging the Dream: Big Band Jazz and the Rebirth of American Culture* (Chicago and London: University of Chicago Press, 1998).

Feather, Leonard. *The Encylopedia of Jazz* (New York: Bonanza Books, 1960).

Fernett, Gene. *A Thousand Golden Horns* (Midland, Michigan: Penile, 1966).

Firestone, Ross. *Swing, Swing, Swing: The Life and Times of Benny Goodman* (London: Hodder and Stoughton, 1993).

Gabbard, Krin. *Jammin' at the Margins: Jazz and the American Cinema* (Chicago and London: University of Chicago Press, 1996).

Gardner, Ava. *Ava: My Story* (New York: Bantam Books, 1990).

Giddins, Gary. *Visions of Jazz: The First Century* (New York and Oxford: Oxford University Press, 1998).

Goodman, Benny and Irving Kolodin. *The Kingdom of Swing* (New York: Frederick Ungar Publishing Company, 1961).

Goldberg, Joe. *Jazz Masters of the Fifties* (London: Collier-Macmillan, 1965).

Goodman, Walter. *The Committee: The Extraordinary Career of the House Committee on Un-American Activities* (New York: Farrar, Straus and Giroux, 1968).

Hall, Fred. *Dialogues in Swing: Intimate Conversations With Stars of the Big Band Era* (Ventura, California: Pathfinder Publishing, 1989).

Hasse, John Edward. *Beyond Category: The Life and Genius of Duke Ellington* (New York: Simon and Schuster, 1993).

Hentoff, Nat. *The Jazz Life* (London: Peter Davies, 1962).

Hirai, Tsuyen. "Homage to Artie Shaw," *The Clarinet* (Summer, 1987), 30–32.

Holiday, Billie and William Dufty. *Lady Sings the Blues* (London: Sphere Books, 1973).

Jacobs, Frank. "Non-Stop Flight: A Reappraisal of the Music of Artie Shaw," *Jazz Journal*. 20 (March 1967), 8–10.

Johnson, James Weldon. *Along This Way: The Autobiography of James Weldon Johnson* (New York: Penguin Books, 1990).

Jones, Maldwyn A. *Destination America* (London: Weidenfeld and Nicholson, 1976).

Kaminsky, Max and V. E. Hughes. *My Life in Jazz* (New York: Harper and Row, 1963).

Kater, Michael H. *Different Drummers: Jazz in the Culture of Nazi Germany* (New York: Oxford University Press, 1992).

Kenney, William H. *Chicago Jazz: A Cultural History, 1904–1930* (New York and Oxford: Oxford University Press, 1993).

Kernfeld, Barry. *The Blackwell Guide to Recorded Jazz* (Oxford: Blackwell Publishers, 1992).

Kraft, James P. *Stage to Studio: Musicians and the Sound Revolution, 1890–1950* (Baltimore and London: The Johns Hopkins University Press, 1996).

Larkin, Philip. *All What Jazz: A Record Diary, 1961–1971* (London: Faber and Faber, 1970, 1985).

Lees, Gene. *Meet Me at Jim and Andy's: Jazz Musicians and Their World* (New York: Oxford University Press, 1988).

———. *Leader of the Band: The Life of Woody Herman* (New York and Oxford: Oxford University Press, 1995).

Leonard, Neil. *Jazz and the White Americans* (Chicago and London: University of Chicago Press, 1963).

Levine, Lawrence W. "Jazz and American Culture," in Levine, *The Unpredictable Past: Explorations in American Cultural History* (New York and Oxford: Oxford University Press, 1993), 172–88.

Meeker, David. *Jazz in the Movies: A Guide to Jazz Musicians, 1917–1977* (London: Talisman Books, 1977).

McCarthy, Albert. *The Dance Band Era: The Dancing Decades From Ragtime to Swing, 1910–1950* (London: Hamlyn, 1971).

McDonough, John. "Artie Shaw: Non-stop Flight From 1938," *Down Beat*, 37 (22 Jan. 1970).

McLeod, Jim. "Artie Shaw: Victim of Success," *Jazz Journal* (April 1994), 12–14; (May 1994), 16–18.

Navasky, Victor S. *Naming Names* (New York: The Viking Press, 1980).

Nicholson, Stuart. *Billie Holiday* (London: Gollancz, 1995).

Nolan, Tom. "Still Cranky After All These Years: Artie Shaw," *Los Angeles* (May 1990), 106–114.

Ostransky, Leroy. *Jazz City: The Impact of Our Cities on the Development of Jazz* (Englewood Cliffs, New Jersey, 1978).

———. *The Anatomy of Jazz* (Seattle: University of Washington Press, 1960).

Peretti, Burton W. *The Creation of Jazz: Music, Race, and Culture in Urban America* (Urbana and Chicago: University of Chicago Press, 1992).

Pessen, Edward. "The Kingdom of Swing: New York City in the Late 1930s," *New York History*, LXX (July 1989), 277–308.

Peterson, Owen. "Artie Shaw" Part I, *Jazz Journal*, 22 (September 1969). 15–17; Part II, *Ibid.* (Oct., 1969), 14–17.

Rothman, Cliff. "Artie Shaw's Solo Beat," *Vanity Fair* (June 1999), 186–228.

Rovere, Richard H. *Senator Joe McCarthy* (London: Methuen, 1960).

Schuller, Gunther. *The Swing Era: The Development of Jazz 1930–1945* (New York: Oxford University Press, 1989).

Shapiro, Nat and Nat Hentoff. *Hear Me Talkin' to Ya: The Story of Jazz By the Men Who Made It* (New York: Rinehart, 1955).

Shaw, Arnold. *52nd Street: The Street of Jazz* (New York: Da Capo Press, 1977).

Shaw, Artie. *I Love You, I Hate You, Drop Dead: Variations on a Theme* (New York: Fleet Publishing Corporation, 1965).

———. *The Best of Intentions and Other Stories* (Santa Barbara, California: John Daniel and Company, 1989).

———. *The Trouble With Cinderella: An Outline of Identity* (New York, Da Capo Press, 1979. Reprint of 1962 edition, with new photographs and a new Introduction).

Shih, Hsio Wen. "The Spread of Jazz and the Big Bands," in *Jazz*, edited by Nat Hentoff and Albert McCarthy (New York: Rinehart and Company, 1959).

Shipton, Alyn. *A New History of Jazz* (New York & London: Continuum, 2001).

Simon, George T. *Simon Says: The Sights and Sounds of the Swing Era, 1935–1955* (New Rochelle, New York: Arlington House, 1971).

———. *The Big Bands* (New York: Macmillan, 1971).

Simosko, Vladimir. "Artie Shaw and His Gramercy Fives," *Journal of Jazz Studies*, 1 (Oct. 1973), 34–56.

Smith, Joe. *Off the Record: An Oral History of Popular Music* edited by Mitchell Fink (London: Sidgwick and Jackson, 1989).

Smith, Willie "The Lion" and George Hoefer. *Music on My Mind: The Memoirs of an American Pianist* (New York: Doubleday, 1964).

Soar, Road. "The Beguine Begins Again," *Jazz Journal*, 37 (Dec. 1984).

———. "Artie Shaw Update," *Jazz Journal*, 40 (Nov. 1987).

Stokes, W. Royal. *The Jazz Scene: An Informal History from New Orleans to 1990* (New York: Oxford University Press, 1991).

Stowe, David W. *Swing Changes: Big Band Jazz in New Deal America* (Cambridge, Mass. and London: Harvard University Press, 1994).

Sudhalter, Richard M. *Lost Chords: White Musicians and their Contributions to Jazz, 1915–1945* (New York: Oxford University Press, 1999).

Taylor, Philip. *The Distant Magnet: European Emigration to the U. S. A.* (London: Eyre and Spottiswoode, 1971).

Taylor, Robert Lewis. "Middle-Aged Man Without a Horn," *The New Yorker*, May 19, 1962.

Tormé, Mel. *It Wasn't All Velvet: An Autobiography* (London: Robson Books, 1989).

———. *Traps The Drum Wonder: The Life of Buddy Rich* (Edinburgh and London: Mainstream Publishing, 1991).

Tracy, Sheila. *Bands, Booze and Broads* (Edinburgh and London: Mainstream Publishing, 1995).

Ulanov, Barry. *Duke Ellington* (London: Musicians Press, 1947).

Vacher, Peter. "Old Man Swing," *Jazz FM*, 12 (1992), 28–9.

Vail, Ken. *Lady Day's Diary: The Life of Billie Holiday 1937–1959* (Chessington, Surrey: Castle Communications, 1996).

Way, Chris. *The Big Bands Go to War* (Edinburgh and London: Mainstream Publishing, 1991).

White, John. *Billie Holiday: Her Life and Times* (Tunbridge Wells: Spellmount and New York: Universe Books, 1987).

Whitlatch, Michael D. *The House Committee on Un-American Activities Entertainment Hearings and their Effects on Performing Arts Careers* Ph.D. Dissertation (Ohio: Bowling Green State University, 1977).

Wilder, Alec. *American Popular Music: The Great Innovators, 1900–1950* (New York: Oxford University Press, 1972).

Willett, Ralph. "Hot Swing and the Dissolute Life: Youth, Style and Popular Music in Europe 1939–49," *Popular Music*, Vol. 8, No.2 (1989), 157–63.

Williams, Martin. *Jazz Heritage* (New York and Oxford: Oxford University Press, 1985).

Yanow, Scott. "Artie Shaw," *Jazziz*, 9, No. 4 (July 1992), 76–105.

Zwerin, Mike. *La Tristesse de Saint Louis: Swing Under the Nazis* (London: Quartet Books, 1985).

Artie Shaw, 1053

INDEX